City Diplomacy

This book examines the theoretical, historical, and practical dimensions of how a city operates internationally. It explores the various approaches of the contentious term "city diplomacy", its impact and follows examples throughout history, the origins of city diplomacy, and its evolution through traditional town-twinning, city networks, and smart cities. Cities have become important actors on the world stage, they have developed diplomatic apparatus and play an important role in securing sustainable futures across a range of key global issues, including climate change, inclusive economic growth, poverty eradication, housing, infrastructure, basic services, productive employment, food security, and public health. Practitioners along with scholars and students of political science, spatial planning, economic geography, international relations, and local government will find this an insightful, invaluable view of the subject.

Antonios M. Karvounis has been working at the Hellenic Republic Ministry of Interior since 2003 as the Head of the Independent Department of International and European Relations and chairman of the inter-ministerial Committee for the international cooperation of the local authorities. Since 2018, he has been a member of the educational staff at the Hellenic Open University, teaching the Modern Greek Administrative System. He studied political science and public administration at Panteion University (PhD, 2019) and the University of Newcastle upon Tyne (PhD, 2003). He is a certified Project Management Professional (PMP)® according to PMI® and is in charge of the book series City Diplomacy at the Ministry of Interior. At the same time, he has published articles and studies on the international activities of local government, as well as, among others, articles and monographs titled *City Diplomacy and the Europeanisation of Local Government: The Prospects of Networking in the Greek Municipalities*, 2023; "City Diplomacy and Public Policy in the Era of COVID-19: Networked Responses from the Greek Capital", *Journal of Public Policy Studies*, Volume 9, Issue 2, 2022, pp. 47–62; "Networks of Solidarity Cities: The Social Dimension of the City Networks within the Europe for Citizens Programme, 2014–2020", *Social Cohesion and Development*, Volume 16, Issue 1, 2021, pp. 61–88; "Paradiplomacy and Social Cohesion: The Case Of The Participation of the Greek Municipalities in European City Networks", *Social Cohesion and Development*, Volume 15, Issue 1, 2020, pp. 81–95; and "The Europeanization of the Local Government in the EU Multi-level Governance System: The City Networking Paradigm and the Greek Case". In E. Van Bever, H. Reynaert and K. Steyvers (Eds.), *The Road to Europe. Main Street or Backward Alley for Local Governments in Europe?* (pp. 211–231). Brugge: Vanden Broele, 2011.

City Diplomacy
An Introduction

Antonios M. Karvounis

Routledge
Taylor & Francis Group

LONDON AND NEW YORK

First published 2025
by Routledge
4 Park Square, Milton Park, Abingdon, Oxon OX14 4RN

and by Routledge
605 Third Avenue, New York, NY 10158

Routledge is an imprint of the Taylor & Francis Group, an informa business

© 2025 Antonios M. Karvounis

British Library Cataloguing-in-Publication Data
A catalogue record for this book is available from the British Library

ISBN: 978-1-032-71633-6 (hbk)
ISBN: 978-1-032-74788-0 (pbk)
ISBN: 978-1-003-47090-8 (ebk)

DOI: 10.4324/9781003470908

Typeset in Times New Roman
by KnowledgeWorks Global Ltd.

To My Sons,

Markos and Constantis

Contents

Introduction

Why This Topic?

Traditionally, studies on international relations and law have paid little attention to cities as global actors. However, cities are widely acknowledged by policymakers, researchers, and urban residents for their crucial role in addressing global challenges and working toward sustainable futures. These challenges encompass a broad spectrum, including climate change, inclusive economic growth, poverty eradication, housing, infrastructure, basic services, productive employment, food security, and public health. Cities are not isolated from these global issues, and their significance in addressing them has been recognized for a long time. For instance, in response to Russia's aggression against Ukraine, the European Alliance of Cities and Regions for the Reconstruction of Ukraine was launched by the Committee of the Regions and its partners, including EU and Ukrainian associations of local and regional authorities, to coordinate their joint efforts directed toward helping the recovery and reconstruction of Ukraine. Between 2013 and 2015, city networks and urban organizations championed the #urbanSDG campaign, advocating for the integration of a dedicated Sustainable Development Goal (SDG), focusing specifically on cities in the post-2015 development agenda. This lobbying endeavor was effective, resulting in the successful inclusion of SDG 11 in the 2030 Agenda for Sustainable Development. SDG 11 emphasizes the significance of sustainable cities and human settlements within the framework of global development goals. Furthermore, the Compact of Mayors, established in 2014, and the Climate Summit for Local Leaders played pivotal roles in mobilizing cities to support an ambitious climate agreement leading up to the United Nations Climate Change Conference (COP21) in Paris in December 2015. As a result, cities gained recognition in the Paris Agreement. Ahead of COP26 in Glasgow in 2021, cities are once again mobilizing through the Cities Race to Zero initiative. In 2017, over 350 mayors and other local leaders in the US took a stand against President Donald Trump's decision to withdraw from the Paris Agreement. Initiatives, such as *Climate Mayors*, *We Are Still In*, and *America's Pledge* brought together these leaders who publicly

DOI: 10.4324/9781003470908-1

committed to achieving their share of emissions reductions. Their commitment and actions played a crucial role in advancing climate progress during President Trump's tenure. From 2016 to 2018, city networks collaborated with academic institutions and United Nations agencies to enhance the role of cities in the Intergovernmental Panel on Climate Change (IPCC). The pinnacle of this collaboration occurred in 2018 at the Edmonton Conference on Cities and Climate Change Science, where the IPCC adopted the Research and Action Agenda for Cities and Climate Change Science. This marked a significant step in recognizing and involving cities in climate change discussions. In 2017, cities established their presence in the G20 ecosystem with the formation of the Urban 20 (U20). Serving as the official city group interacting with the G20, the U20 brings an urban perspective to the G20 discussions and advocates for ambitious and equitable climate action. In 2019, cities once again united to create "For cities by cities: Key Takeaways for City Decision Makers from the IPCC 1.5°C Report" and "Summary for Urban Policymakers". These initiatives aimed to distill and communicate crucial insights from the IPCC 1.5°C Report, offering valuable information for city decision-makers and policymakers dealing with climate-related issues. Additionally, increased interaction between international organizations and cities is evident, exemplified by the UN Special Envoy on Cities and Climate Change and cities' participation in global compacts and legal agreements with institutions, such as the World Bank. Thus the assertion that "nations talk, cities act", often attributed to various city leaders, encapsulates the proactive stance of cities in global politics. Cities should not be viewed merely as passive venues for international relations or subordinate to higher politics.

Given this context, it is evident that cities are integral players in the international arena. Cities have evolved into significant actors on the world stage, developing diplomatic apparatus and engaging in increasingly professional diplomatic activities. In this respect, city diplomacy refers to the way cities pursue their interests internationally with political actors, often through networking with other cities. This can occur bilaterally, multilaterally, regionally, or transnationally. In short, city diplomacy influences global and national agendas to promote local interests; provides unique access to the knowledge and resources of peer cities, fostering mutual benefits; enables cities to garner recognition and support for their leadership, ambition, and innovation, both internationally and domestically.

While though city diplomacy is on the rise, challenges exist. During the Cold War, cities' international relations were primarily limited to peer-to-peer cooperation. However, there has been a shift toward more explicitly entrepreneurial, public-private "hybrid" urban policies, reminiscent of pre-modern city-states. Traditional twinning organizations, such as Sister Cities International (SCI), have broadened their focus from specific city-to-city cooperation to a more extensive concept of "city diplomacy", involving interactions between cities and various non-municipal actors. City networks, including organizations, such as SCI, have evolved beyond twinning, emphasizing strategy and alliance capability. These networks now engage with actors beyond municipal governments, collaborating with entities, such as the UN, the World Bank, the EU, and increasingly intertwining with the cross-national activities of the private sector. In some instances, the private sector takes the lead in initiating city networking efforts, as seen in the cases of the Rockefeller Foundation's 100 Resilient Cities Network and Cisco's City Protocol. At the same time, city diplomacy takes multiple forms other than mere collaboration or advocacy. Place branding, smart cities practices apply to city diplomacy. Consequently, cities can utilize traditional types of city diplomacy, such as town-twinnings or city networks as well as modern tools, such as branding and smart cities diplomacy to advance their local interests and enhance their international image while activating their power to impact global policies.

The Aim of the Book

This book intends to provide the reader with the current theoretical and practical aspects of city diplomacy, bringing together insights about its various forms, traditional and modern ones, from practitioners' viewpoints to academic perspectives. Thus the topics of the book range from the basic framework of discussion about city diplomacy to the practicalities and its impact at local level. We hope this work will encourage scholars to turn their attention to urban centers as active agents in international scene, making use more and advanced ways to conduct city diplomacy.

The Structure of the Book

The book consists of three parts. The first part of the book, *The Framework of City Diplomacy*, includes four chapters that shed light on the conceptual, historical, and institutional aspects of city diplomacy. Chapter 1, reviewing the relevant literature, is divided into three sections. The first section traces the historical path of paradiplomacy studies. The second section explores the various arguments around paradiplomacy regarding contested concepts, its various manifestations, its relation with national foreign policy as well as the related goals and instruments. And the final section examines the role of city diplomacy in the paradiplomacy debate. Chapter 2 delves into the results of the research on city diplomacy; explores the various definitions of the concept; and examines its diverse goals, actors, and tools. Chapter 3 introduces the historical trajectory of city diplomacy. It is divided into three sections arranged in chronological order. The first section considers the ancient roots of the modern city diplomacy till the advent of the nation-state. The second section provides us with historical knowledge on city diplomacy from the Peace of Westphalia till the modern era of city partnerships in the first quarter of the 20th century. The last section is focused on the contemporary period since the World War II. Chapter 4 explores the international, European, and national trends of the legal environment in which cities operate internationally. Part II includes four chapters that present the traditional and recent forms of city diplomacy. In fact, Chapter 5 outlines, first, a historical account and a conceptual framework of town-twinnings; it then explores the success factors and the practicalities to set up a town-twinning partnership. Chapter 6 examines city networking as a major form of city diplomacy through its historical, theoretical, and practical aspects. City branding is the main topic of Chapter 7 which is divided into four sections. The first one introduces the terminology coined and used in the relevant literature. The second identifies the relationship of city branding with the soft power of city diplomacy. The third section, building upon the previous discussions, presents the main synergies between them in the cultural and economic domains. Finally, the fourth section links city branding activities with the internationalization strategy of the local authorities and underlines the main conditions for enhancing city's international distinctiveness. Chapter 8 discusses the concept of smart city as well as the various ways in which smart city and city diplomacy can be combined. The last part of the book includes two chapters, exploring the practicalities of city diplomacy. Chapter 9 describes the analytical steps needed to put city diplomacy into practice in a more project management frame, whereas Chapter 10 explores the theoretical approaches and the various narratives of city diplomacy's impact, along with the intermediate variables.

Part I

The Framework of City Diplomacy

1 Paradiplomacy

1.1 Introduction

Traditional diplomacy was initially an exclusive competence held by the official state structures of foreign affairs, a reflection of the international system in which states were the sole actors entitled to engage in international relations. Many of these practices were codified in the Vienna Convention on Diplomatic Relations (1961) and the Vienna Convention on Consular Relations (1963). In recent years, the scope of diplomacy has broadened significantly (Karvounis, 2023, p. 51). Traditionally focused on timeless issues, such as peace and war, diplomacy now encompasses a wide array of topics, including international security, economy, technology, scientific developments, education, and the arts (Keohane and Nye, 1989, pp. 26–27). Notably, political scientist Hans Morgenthau observed three decades ago that diplomacy was losing vitality, with its functions declining to an unprecedented extent in the history of the modern state system (Morgenthau, 1993, p. 367). The international arena has also seen an increase in protagonists, with non-state organizations challenging the dominance of nation-states. Contemporary diplomacy thus exhibits paradoxical trends. On the one hand, there's increasing internationalization as national governments respond to various international relations, economic interdependence, and unmanageable demands within their political systems. On the other hand, there's vigilance from subnational interests, states, and non-state agents against these pressures, as their consequences become visible domestically. In this context, regionalism aims to enhance, rather than reject, foreign policy by involving a variety of subnational actors in pursuing their goals at the international level. Hocking (1993, p. 18) argues that, similar to firms forming strategic alliances for cost and competitiveness, "regions and cities develop international relationships and alliances to strengthen their position in the global economy".

In the early 1960s, Butler introduced the concept of "paradiplomacy" to describe "personal or parallel diplomacy complementing or competing with the regular foreign policy of the government" (Butler, 1962, p. 13). Paradiplomacy refers to the direct and relatively autonomous international activities

DOI: 10.4324/9781003470908-3

of subnational actors (such as regions and cities) that pursue policies parallel to, coordinated with, complementary to, and sometimes conflicting with their central governments' diplomacy (Duchacek et al., 1988; Soldatos, 1990). In this respect, this chapter, reviewing the relevant literature, is divided into three sections. The first section traces the historical path of paradiplomacy studies. The second section explores the various arguments around paradiplomacy regarding contested concepts, its various manifestations, its relation with national foreign policy as well as the related goals and instruments. And the final section examines the role of city diplomacy in the paradiplomacy debate.

1.2   The Historical Path of the Paradiplomatic Studies

Kuznetsov (2015, p. 43) notes that the 1970s were a period of the "genesis of paradiplomacy studies". Nevertheless, the real progress in the quality of paradiplomacy studies came to light during the 1980s, when a group of North American political scientists, including Ivo Duchacek, Hans Michelmann, John Kincaid, Panayotis Soldatos, Earl Fry, and others, in addition to providing a narrative of regional international activity, also attempted to conceptualize the phenomenon of paradiplomacy and tried to create some explanatory theoretical patterns to understand the causes and consequences of constituent diplomacy for federal systems (Duchacek, 1984; Fry, 1989; Kincaid, 1990; Michelmann, 1989; Soldatos, 1990; Soldatos and Michelmann, 1992). In the 1990s, global changes in world politics, such as the fall of the Iron Curtain and the high-speed strengthening of the European Union as a new supranational regime, drastically increased the role of subnational entities in many parts of the globe, particularly in Europe and in new post-communist federations, such as Russia (Aguirre, 1999; Aldecoa and Keating, 1999; Borras-Alomar et al., 1994; Hocking, 1999; Keating, 1999; Stern, 1994). The activities in the international arena of the Basque Country and Catalonia in Spain, Flandreau and Wallonia in Belgium, Tatarstan in Russia and other regions attracted much attention from European researchers, and as a result, paradiplomacy studies expanded outside North American academia. The concept of the "Europe of the Regions" became dominant in the European discourse at that time and brought more recognition to the idea of high diversity in Europe at the subnational level (Aguirre, 1999; Aldecoa and Keating, 1999; Borras-Alomar et al., 1994; Hocking, 1999; Keating, 1999). In the 2000s, scholarly interest in paradiplomacy geographically spread worldwide, and the field gained its new academic stalwarts among researchers from Latin America and Asia (Zhimin, 2005; Zhu, 2005). It is especially interesting to mention the publication by Jain Rurnedra in 2005 of the monograph titled *Japan's Subnational Governments in International Affairs* (Rundera, 2005). The innovatory component of this work consists of the fact that it breaks away from the rather strong prepossession in the literature of the previous decades that the phenomenon of paradiplomacy is an attribute of federal or quasi-federal states, such as Canada or Spain, but not common for unitary nations, such as Japan. Kuznetsov (2015) categorizes paradiplomacy into 11 dimensions: Constitutional, Federalist, Nationalist, International Relations, Border, Globalization, Security/Geopolitical, Global Economy, Environmental, Diplomacy, and Separatist/Non-recognized States. These dimensions encompass legal, federalist, nationalist, and global aspects, exploring paradiplomacy's impact on security, economics, environment, diplomacy, and recognition of non-recognized states.

Despite the variety of paradiplomacy studies (Karvounis, 2020), paradiplomacy research agenda has been very constructive in conceptualizing the external activities of subnational authorities and in making descriptive inventories of paradiplomatic activities and instruments. Lecours argues that the paradiplomacy literature mostly suffers from two weaknesses: "The absence of a general theoretical perspective that can explain how regional governments have acquired international agency, and what shapes their foreign policy, international relations and negotiating behaviour; the second is a lack of focus on constructing general analytical frameworks that can guide the study of paradiplomacy" (Lecours, 2002, p. 92). At the same time, though, paradiplomacy can serve many different purposes and presents potential opportunities. An overview of the paradiplomacy literature below confirms that evaluation.

1.3   Concept, Forms, and Goals of Paradiplomacy

First, scholars employ various concepts to analyze paradiplomacy, initially defined by Duchacek (1990) and Soldatos (1990, 1993) as international actions by subnational actors challenging or complementing nation-states. In fact, Duchacek introduced "protodiplomacy" for subnational efforts in separatist objectives. Cornago (2013, p. 40) later defined paradiplomacy as sub-state governments' engaging in international relationships to promote socioeconomic, cultural, or political issues. Some distinguish paradiplomacy from "protodiplomacy" (Nossal et al., 2015), the latter aiming for international recognition and independence. In Quebec, there have been sporadic episodes of protodiplomacy, such as the one in the late 1970s and mid-1990s. However, at present, the international activities of the provincial government aimed at ensuring against the independence for Quebec as a sovereign state, but a paradiplomacy that strengthens Québécois identity. According to Kuznetsov (2015), paradiplomacy refers to the involvement of constituent units (regions, provinces, autonomous communities, Länder) in international affairs, whereas Aldecoa (1999) introduces "plurinational diplomacy", emphasizing sub-state actors' influence on state foreign policies. Kincaid introduced "constituent diplomacy", underlining the role of regions, provinces, etc. On the other hand, Hocking (1993) challenges these terms, considering that the concepts of paradiplomacy or protodiplomacy were created to strengthen distinctions and disputes between central and non-central governments. Instead, he views diplomacy as a complex, interconnected system within a state structure (Lequesne and Paquin, 2017, p. 190).

Second, Ivo Duchacek (1990, pp. 15–27) identifies three different forms of paradiplomacy. First, cross-border regional paradiplomacy refers to cross-border contacts – institutional, formal, and above all, informal contacts – that are determined by geographical proximity and nature of common problems and their possible solutions. Second, trans-regional paradiplomacy refers to connections and negotiations among non-central governments who are not neighbors, but whose national governments are. Finally, global paradiplomacy consists of political-functional contacts with distant nations that connect non-central governments, not only with commercial, industrial, or cultural centers in other continents, but also with different branches or agencies of foreign national governments. Besides, Hocking (1993) used the term "multi-layered diplomacy", arguing that sub-state governments participate in a wide and complex diplomatic network with several levels or layers of governments and other actors, both inside and outside of their domestic system. Kincaid (1990, 2001) prefers, as seen above, the term "constituent diplomacy", arguing that concepts, such as paradiplomacy or subnational diplomacy, imply that the external activities of sub-state governments are inferior or supplemental to national diplomacy; since subnational authorities legitimately represent the interests of their constituents and have powers to conduct international activities in the areas where they are competent, their external actions are to be labeled constituent diplomacy. In this respect, it is in the best interest of national governments to support subnational authorities to actively participate internationally, since they are in direct contact with the people and more accurately represent their interests (Schiavon, 2019, p. 7).

Third, inevitably, the debate on paradiplomacy has centered on whether these international activities provide support or threaten the national conduction of foreign policy. The term "paradiplomacy" can be interpreted in accordance with the Greek etymology of the prefix "para" as a process which only resembles diplomacy, functions in a way similar to it, but at the same time is outside its scope (Surmacz, 2018). In this perspective, paradiplomacy becomes para-diplomacy. Both interpretations create a picture of two "paths" of diplomacy: the central one in which states operate and the peripheral one for sub-state actors. As seen above, Aldecoa (1999) has argued for "plurinational diplomacy" to explain the evolution of the international activities of the subnational authorities in multicultural states, especially in the EU, in the framework of regional integration. The subnational authorities are not just participants in the international activities, but aspire also to become influencers of the national foreign policies. Cornago (2010) notes that subnational authorities have innovative processes that generate their own institutions and practices, challenging thus the traditional diplomacy. In the same wavelength, Criekemans (2010) analyzes how the international actions of the subnational authorities that enjoy considerable constitutional powers, such as those in

Belgium, Canada, and Spain can be very similar to those of the national governments, making difficult to differentiate one from the other (Schiavon, ibid.). Likewise, Kuznetsov (2015, p. 87) considers that paradiplomacy is depicted as a process that has a universal character and is inherent to all types of nations to a certain degree. Also the boundaries between diplomacy and paradiplomacy have become blurred since the latter's practices and activities are widespread around the world (Cornago, 2010). Lecours (2008, pp. 6–7) argues that in order to minimize potential issues of incoherence in foreign policy, Western states, where at least one region developed a significant paradiplomacy, have crafted channels and mechanisms of intergovernmental consultation and coordination. In Canada, where provinces play a formal role in the implementation of international treaties, consultation surrounding the definition of Canadian positions on matters of provincial jurisdiction takes place within sectoral intergovernmental forums. Typically, discussions of international issues occur in yearly meetings of federal and provincial ministers. In Belgium, where the competencies of regional governments in international relations are a matter of constitutional law, arrangements are more formalized. For Belgium to take an international position (including treatysigning) in an area of jurisdiction that is domestically the Region's or the Community's, the relevant regional government needs to provide its endorsement. This is an interlocking system that gives a veto to all the actors involved in an international process or issue as a result of constitutionally specified powers. On the contrary, Basque paradiplomacy remains fairly conflictual in terms of the relationship between the Basque government and the central state, because it is seen by many Spanish politicians as challenging the unity of the country.

Fourth, the international activities of the subnational authorities are guided by a variety of objectives and economic, political, social, and political goals (Michelmann, 2009). Lecours (2008, p. 2) underlines three layers of paradiplomacy: economic issues as a function of global economic competition; cooperation (cultural, educational, technical, technological, etc.); and political considerations. For instance, American states' international activity consists essentially of the pursuit of economic interests. At the cooperation level, Baden-Württemberg has been a leader in the creation of the "Four Motors of Europe" and the Assembly of European Regions. In the case of political goals, Quebec, Flanders, Catalonia, and the Basque Country seek to develop a set of international relations that will affirm the cultural distinctiveness, political autonomy, and the national character of the community they represent. True, according to Schiavon (2019, p. 8) and Tavares (2016, pp. 40–47), subnational authorities' motivations can also be of political nature, such as advancing local autonomy or even preparing for national secession or independence, promoting decentralization, attracting political attraction during election campaigns. In other cases, the subnational authorities desire to influence regional or global policy debates in issues or areas in which they are particularly interested, such as regional integration, climate change, sustainable development, and human rights. Furthermore, these goals can be more pragmatic, addressing cross-border or regional issues, such as trade, infrastructure, investment, migration, and the environment (Schiavon, ibid.). The strength of the trend has led the Economic Forum in its *2014 The Competitiveness of Cities* report to advocate that "cities should create their own (foreign) policies on trade, FDI, tourism and attracting foreign talent and advance these globally as far as possible" (Tavares, 2016, p. 28). However, the above contributions fail to formulate hypotheses with respect to what kind of circumstances lead to what kind of paradiplomacy. Keating (1999, pp. 1, 13) treated paradiplomacy as an empirical phenomenon whose variation needs to be explained. He suggests multiple answers to the question "why do regions go abroad?", pointing to economic (seeking trade and investment), cultural (seeking support in the international arena for language and culture), and political reasons (seeking recognition and legitimacy as something more than regions).

Finally, the instruments of local authorities' paradiplomacy are diverse and evolve over time (see Part II). As a multilayered term, paradiplomacy can be more steered by image than content in more ceremonial, image-building, and public relations activities, such as town-twinnings, probably the most prolific instrument available to subnational authorities in their foreign activities. In contrast to the ceremonial paradiplomacy, subnational authorities participate in international and regional networks and organizations. Furthermore, they conduct public diplomacy, receive visitors from around the world, and organize international events; they also travel to foreign countries in trade and investment missions, to strengthen relations with the diaspora, to conclude cooperation agreements or memoranda of understanding, or to participate in regional and global summits and meetings (Schiavon, 2019, p. 8). These instruments raise the question whether cities can be included within the paradiplomacy studies.

1.4   Paradiplomacy and City Diplomacy

As Marchetti (2021) rightly argues, the phenomenon of city diplomacy struggles to find a place in the traditional theoretical framework of international relations and paradiplomacy debate. Concerning the international relations theory, liberals, such as Keohane and Nye (1989), questioned the traditional paradigm of international relations, in which state and interstate relations are the only components in world politics. For them world politics is not a system of political relations between states, but rather *political interactions between any "significant actors" whose characteristics include autonomy, the control of substantial resources relevant to a given issue area and participation in political relationship across state lines.* Paradiplomacy of cities and regions, seen through the liberal lenses, is a logical consequence of the major changes in the international system: the diminishing role of interstate relations, the evanescing difference between "high" and "low" politics, as well as the democratization and modernization that allows linking state loyalty with local or regional levels. The realist school of international relations looks at paradiplomacy of cities and regions in, quite obviously, a different way than liberals. Realists do not believe that the state-centered paradigm of global politics is either out of date or explain adequately world affairs. The will to maximize the national interests of the state is still the most important force that shapes the global landscape (Waltz, 1979). Realists have noticed the emergence of new transnational players in the world politics, but do not perceive them as autonomous powers. Paradiplomatic activities of regions and cities, when looking through realist lenses, are no more than effects of "the rationalisation of the foreign policy of central national governments, which consider regional authorities' activities abroad beneficial rather than noxious tendency for state interests" (Kuznetsov, 2015). For the constructivists, state behavior is influenced by intersubjective structures rather than material capabilities. Intersubjectivity is constituted by collective meaning systems in which states participate and which they reproduce through their practices. Sovereignty is the single most important intersubjective structure. Similarly to the concept of identity or interests it has been constructed by political and cultural elites (Wendt, 1999). Paradiplomacy of cities and regions appears in the works of constructivists mainly in the context of constructing regional identity as a state. Summing up, for social constructivists paradiplomacy is interesting in the context of a region's or city's pursuit of sovereign statehood and not as a functional response to globalization and economic interdependence (liberal approach) or merely as an instrument of a state's foreign policy (realist approach).

Apart from the international relations theory, there are also doubts about cities' role in paradiplomacy. Some researchers, such as Kuznetsov (2015) or Cornago (2010), argue that there is a "principal dissemblance" between regional and local levels of governance. The latter, unlike regions, are not part of state power and their nature is different. As Kuznetsov states:

> In other words, the Canadian province of Alberta can be considered as a non-sovereign state actor in international affairs, but the capital of the province, Edmonton, should be viewed as a non-sovereign and non-state actor in its external performances. The only exception can be applied to those municipal bodies that occupy a place in state hierarchy right after the central government, and, as such, they are recognized on legal bases as "regions" in their power competence, for example, the two Russian "federal cities," Moscow and Saint-Petersburg.

However, the paradiplomatic phenomenon has been growing and involves, not only governments in federations, but also governments of global cities, such as London, Tokyo, New York, and Shanghai (Scott, 2001; Tavares, 2016). In this view, the international activities of non-central governments must be put into a broader global perspective as an intensive, extensive, and permanent phenomenon. Benjamin Barber (2013) convincingly presents this political phenomenon of the growing importance of cities in his book *If Mayors Ruled the World. Dysfunctional Nations, Rising Cities.* Many other researchers (Van der Pluijm and Mellisen, 2007) conceptualize "city diplomacy" as a form of decentralizing international relations management, with cities being the key actors. As far as motives, methods, and other determinants of their engagement in the external relations, they are similar to those of regions.

Due to this fact there is not much sense in excluding cities from an analysis of paradiplomacy. Both cities and regions can be labeled as "non central government units" and both can act as separate political actors, competing and cooperating with state authorities and each other. Their ability to be actors of paradiplomacy depends in practice, not only on their legal status, but rather on the resources they command, political will of leaders, level of autonomy within the state, and nature of relations between the city as well as regional and central governments. Those factors are very much the same in the case of regional and municipal authorities. Due to this fact, cities cannot be excluded.

1.5   Conclusions

After reviewing the literature on paradiplomacy, we can safely conclude that paradiplomacy has undoubtedly aided researchers of international relations and comparative politics to learn more about the international initiatives of cities and regions. The concept of paradiplomacy has been used in literature to produce a number of helpful and intriguing conceptualizations and inventory of paradiplomatic tools and activities. We now have a good understanding of what paradiplomacy is and how city diplomacy fits into it. In this sense, the development of a paradiplomacy necessarily involves domestic adjustments. Within a city or region, paradiplomacy involves establishing structures to give directions to international action and administer programs, and some channels (or exploiting existing ones in new ways) with the central government to exchange information and coordinate action.

References

Aguirre, I. (1999) "Making Sense of Paradiplomacy: An Intertextual Enquiry about a Concept in Search of a Definition", *Regional and Federal Studies*, 9 (1), Spring, pp. 185–209.

Aldecoa, F. (1999) "Towards Plurinational Diplomacy in the Deeper and Wider European Union (1985–2005)". In F. Aldecoa and M. Keating (Eds.) *Paradiplomacy in Action: The Foreign Relations of Sub-National Governments* (pp. 82–94). London: Frank Cass.

Aldecoa, F., and Keating, M. (1999) "Introduction". In A. Aldecoa and M. Keating (Eds.) *Paradiplomacy in Action. The Foreign Relations of Subnational Governments* (pp. vii–x). London: Frank Cass Publishers.

Barber, B.R. (2013) *If Mayors Ruled the World. Dysfunctional Nations, Rising Cities*, New Haven & London: Yale University Press.

Borras-Alomar, S., Christiansen, T., and Rodriguez- Poze, A. (1994) "Towards a 'Europe of the Regions': Visions and Reality from a Critical Perspective", *Regional Politics and Policy*, 4 (2), pp. 27–59.

Butler, R. (1962). "Paradiplomacy". In A.O. Sarkissian (Ed.), *Studies in Diplomatic History and Historiography in Honour of G. P. Gooch, C.H.* New York: Barnes and Noble.

Cornago, N. (2010) "On the Normalization of Sub-State Diplomacy", *The Hague Journal of Diplomacy*, 5 (1–2), pp. 11–36.

Cornago, N. (2013) *Plural Diplomacies. Normative Predicaments and Functional Imperatives*, Leiden–Boston: Martinus Nijhoff Publishers.

Criekemans, D. (2010) *Foreign Policy and Diplomacy of the Belgian Regions: Flanders and Wallonia*, The Hague: Netherlands Institute of International Relations Clingendael.

Duchacek, I. (1984) "The International Dimension of Subnational Self-Government", *Publius*, 14 (4), Autumn, pp. 5–31.

Duchacek, I.D. (1990) "Perforated Sovereignties: Towards a Typology of New Actors in International Relations". In H. Michelmann and P. Soldatos (Eds.) *Federalism and International Relations: The Role of Subnational Units* (pp. 1–33). New York: Oxford University Press.

Duchacek, I.D., Latouche, D., and Stevenson, G. (1988) *Perforated Sovereignties and International Relations: Trans-sovereign Contacts of Subnational Governments*, Westport: Westport University Press.

Fry, E. (1989) "The New International Cities Era: The Global Linkages of North American Cities with Emphasis on Los Angeles and San Francisco". In E. Fry, L. Radebaugh and P. Soldatos (Eds.) *The New International Cities Era* (pp. 5–36). Provo: Brigham Young University Press.

Hocking, B. (1993) *Localising Foreign Policy. Non-Central Governments and Multilayered Diplomacy*, New York: St. Martin's Press.

Hocking, B. (1999) "Patrolling the 'Frontier': Globalisation, Localization and the 'Actorness' of Non-Central Governments", *Regional and Federal Studies*, 9 (1), pp. 17–39.

Karvounis, A. (2020) "Paradiplomacy and Social Cohesion: The Case of the Participation of the Greek Municipalities in European City Networks", *Social Cohesion and Development*, 15 (1), pp. 81–95.

Karvounis, A. (2023) *City Diplomacy and the Europeanisation of Local Government. The Prospects of Networking in the Greek Municipalities*, Cham: Palgrave Macmillan.

Keating, M. (1999) *The New Regionalism in Western Europe. Territorial Restructuring and Political Change*, Cheltenham: Edward Elgar.

Keohane, R., and Nye, J. (1989) *Power and Interdependence*, New York: Harper Collins.

Kincaid, J. (1990) "Constituent Diplomacy in Federal Polities and the Nation-State: Conflict and Co-Operation". In H. Michelmann and P. Soldatos (Eds.) *Federalism and International Relations: The Role of Subnational Units* (pp. 54–75). Oxford: Oxford University Press.

Kincaid, J. (2001) "The State of US Federalism, 2000–2001: Continuity in Crisis", *Publius: The Journal of Federalism*, 33, pp. 145–162.

Kuznetsov, A.S. (2015) *Theory and Practice of Paradiplomacy. Subnational Governments in International Affairs*, New York: Routledge.

Lecours, A. (2002) "Paradiplomacy: Reflections on the Foreign Policy and International Relations of Regions", *International Negotiation*, 7, pp. 91–114.

Lecours, A.. (2008) *Political Issues of Paradiplomacy: Lessons from the Developed World*, The Hague: Netherlands Institute of International Relations Clingendael.

Lequesne, C., and Paquin, S. (2017) "Federalism, Paradiplomacy and Foreign Policy: A Case of Mutual Neglect", *International Negotiation*, 22, pp. 183–204.

Marchetti, R. (2021) *City Diplomacy. From City-States to Global Cities*, Ann Arbor: University Michigan Press.

Michelmann, H. (1989) "Calgary: A Nascent International City". In E. Fry, L. Radebaugh and P. Soldatos (Eds.) *The New International Cities Era* (pp. 161–184). Provo: Brigham Young University Press.

Michelmann, H. (2009) *Foreign Relations in Federal Countries*, Montreal: McGill-Queen's University Press.

Morgenthau, H. (1993) *Politics among Nations. The Struggle for Power and Peace*, 7th edition, New York: McGraw-Hill.

Nossal, K.R., Roussell, S., and Paquin, S. (2015) *The Politics of Canadian Foreign Policy*, Montreal: McGill-Queen's University Press.

Pluijm, R., and Melissen, J. (2007) "City Diplomacy: The Expanding Role of Cities in International Relations", *Discussion Papers on Diplomacy*, The Hague: Netherlands Institute of International Relations Clingendael.

Rundera, J. (2005) *Japan's Subnational Governments in International Affairs*, Oxon: Routledge.

Schiavon, J. (2019) *Comparative Paradiplomacy*, New York: Routledge.

Scott, A.J. (2001) "Introduction". In A.J. Scott (Ed.) *Global City-Regions. Trends, Theory, Policy*. Oxford-New York: Oxford University Press.

Soldatos, P. (1990) "An Explanatory Framework for the Study of Federated States as Foreign Policy Actors". In H. Michelmann and P. Soldatos (Eds.) *Federalism and International Relations. The Role of Subnational Units* (pp. 34–53). Oxford: Clarendon Press.

Soldatos, P. (1993) "Cascading Subnational Paradiplomacy in an Interdependent and Transnational World". In D. Brown and E. Fry (Eds.) *States and Provinces in the International Political Economy*, Berkeley: Institute of Governmental Studies (IGS), 2, pp. 45–64.

Soldatos, P., and Michelmann, H. (1992) "Subnational Units' Paradiplomacy in the Context of European Integration", *Journal of European Integration*, 15 (2–3), Winter, pp. 129–134.

Stern, J. (1994) "Moscow Meltdown: Can Russia Survive?", *International Security*, 18 (4), Spring, pp. 40–65.

Surmacz, B. (2018) "City Diplomacy", *Barometr Regionalny*, 16 (1), pp. 7–18.

Tavares, R. (2016) *Paradiplomacy – Cities and States as Global Players*, New York: Oxford University Press.

Waltz, K. (1979) *Theory of International Politics*, New York: McGraw Hill.

Wendt, A. (1999) *Social Theory of International Politics*, Cambridge: Cambridge University Press.

Zhimin, C. (2005) "Coastal Provinces and China's Foreign Policy Making". In Y. Hao and L. Su (Eds.) *China's Foreign Policy Making: Societal Force and Chinese American Policy* (pp. 187–207). Burlington: Ashgate Publishing Limited.

Zhu, Z. (2005) "Regional Influence in China's US Policy Making: The Roles of Shanghai and Wang Daohan". In Y. Hao and L. Su (Eds.) *China's Foreign Policy Making: Societal Force and Chinese American Policy* (pp. 209–227). Burlington: Ashgate Publishing Limited.

2 City Diplomacy

2.1 Introduction

Cities are now more connected than ever before on a global scale. Yet local governments are not just spectators of this networked age: they are actively forging links across borders, taking part in setting the international agenda, and shifting the landscape of urban politics from local to increasingly global. There are hundreds of formalized city networks around the world addressing a broad range of issues, and the potential of cities' external engagements is as vast as it is untapped. City diplomacy becomes a strategic activity for cities worldwide if they are to remain relevant in the new global order (Curtis and Acuto, 2018). In broad terms, city diplomacy is the conduct of external relations undertaken by official representatives of cities with other actors, particularly other cities, nation-states, universities, NGOs, and corporations. Today, city diplomacy has become more than a symbolic relationship or cultural exchange, and cities are increasingly recognized in their potential to shape international processes and global agendas (Karvounis, 2022). Furthermore, the boundaries of cities are blurred as borough, municipal, metropolitan, and regional authorities see the benefit of engaging globally and representing their domains on international stage. City diplomacy is increasingly formal. A recent UCL City Leadership Lab study of 200 city networks found that a quarter met at least once a year, with another 20% scheduling irregular meetings and conferences. More than 44% of the city networks have produced joint policies. Indeed, as evidenced by groups, such as the C40 Cities Climate Leadership Group, the Global Covenant of Mayors for Climate & Energy, ICLEI-Local Governments for Sustainability, and the Rockefeller Foundation's 100 Resilient Cities, city networks have massive potential to help cities mobilize resources, shape global agendas, and connect urban innovation across the world. Yet there are mounting concerns that resource-constrained cities could be overwhelmed by the multitude of twinning and network arrangements available to them. To take full advantage of the growing cadre of city diplomacy opportunities, cities must work to better navigate the global landscape of urban networks and understand how local governments are

DOI: 10.4324/9781003470908-4

building capacity to support international engagement activities. As such, city diplomacy represents a practice and a research topic at the crossroads of local and international affairs. In this respect, this chapter explores the various definitions of the concept and examines the diverse drivers, goals, actors, and tools of city diplomacy.

2.2   Definitions of City Diplomacy

As a subset of paradiplomacy, there are a few definitions of the concept of "city diplomacy". In fact, the above concept has never been seriously elaborated and described. Most of the definitions given to city diplomacy are functional and limited only to the activities of cities (Wang and Amiri, 2019). The definitions mainly come from specific organizations and international associations of cities that are active in promoting these actions. Scholarly attention to the concept emerged in the 1990s within the debate over paradiplomacy (Aldecoa and Keating, 1999; Hocking, 1993; Soldatos, 1990). In the US, the study of city diplomacy was confined to the social protests against the neoliberal policies of the Reagan era, whereas in Europe, the concept was part of the discussions on decentralized cooperation (Le Galès, 2002).

More specifically, in 2008, in Recommendation no. 234, the Congress of Local and Regional Authorities of the Council of Europe defined city diplomacy as "a tool of local governments and their associations to promote social cohesion, prevention of conflict, conflict resolution and post-conflict reconstruction in order to create a stable environment in which citizens can live together in a state of peace, democracy and prosperity" (Congress of Local and Regional Authorities, 2008). In its Resolution no. 251 (2008), the Congress argued that city diplomacy expresses the growing importance of the city as a political actor on the international stage. In the same year, the 1st World Conference on City Diplomacy was organized by the international network of the United Cities and Local Governments (UCLG), the International Cooperation Service of the Association of Dutch Municipalities (VNG), and the Municipality of The Hague. The conference was held in The Hague (11–13 June 2008), following the relevant preparatory conferences in Perugia (2006) and Barcelona (2007). It adopted the Hague Agenda for City Diplomacy, which referred to the Council of Europe's definition (VNG, 2008). A year later, the Committee of the Regions (CoR), in the Opinion of Nicosia city councilor, Ms. Eleni Loukaidou, adopted a similar definition during its 78th Plenary Session: City diplomacy "is broadly defined as the tool of local governments and their agencies for the global promotion of social cohesion, a sustainable environment, conflict prevention, conflict resolution and post-conflict reconstruction, with the aim of creating a stable environment within which citizens can coexist peacefully in a climate of democracy, progress and prosperity" (Committee of the Regions, 2009). The CoR argued that "modern diplomacy is no longer expressed and practiced only by national governments, but, given the need for dialogue, cooperation and coordination to achieve the goals of peace, democracy and respect for human rights at all levels, closer cooperation between national governments and local and regional authorities is a natural, but also necessary direction for a multi-level and more effective approach and strategy". In fact, the CoR underlined that "cities and megacities play an important role in international cooperation since they cooperate with other municipalities in international networks". Similarly, the Glocal Forum, founded in 2001 in Zurich with headquarters in Rome, emphasized the role of local authorities in the world governance system and described city diplomacy as a form of decentralization of international relations management in which municipalities are seen as protagonists, particularly in war-torn regions. Although the Federation of Canadian Municipalities does not define city diplomacy in this way, it also approaches the international role of local authorities in terms of war and peace (Bush, 2003). The above definitions are examples of extremely restrictive approaches that focus on issues of security (conflict prevention, peace processes, post-conflict reconstruction actions), cooperation with developing countries, culture, and entrepreneurship. In the same vein, the Institute of International Relations of the Netherlands distinguished six dimensions of city diplomacy: security, development, economy, culture, networks, and representation (Van der Pluijm and Melissen, 2007, pp. 19–33). According to the Institute, city diplomacy can be defined as "the institutions and processes by which cities engage in cooperation with actors in the international political arena in order to represent their interests vis-à-vis others".

On the other hand, Acuto and Rayner (2016, p. 1148), analyzing city networking activities, put city diplomacy on a wider basis as "mediated 'international' relations between rightful representatives of polities (cities in this instance) that result in agreements, collaborations, further institution-building and cooperation across boundaries". Indeed, according to Sizoo (2007, pp. 6–8), cities play different roles in the international arena: as lobbyists, lobbying international organizations, while promoting and defending the interests and concerns of their residents; as mediators, negotiated agreements between local authorities; and as partners in projects, participating together with other local authorities to promote or implement specific policies. La Porte (2011, p. 8) suggests that city diplomats' initiatives mirror traditional diplomats or international representatives. They gather information, enhance understanding of global developments, represent their region, engage in international organizations and events, negotiate agreements with other cities, and take actions to prevent conflicts and implement peace agreements. In this sense, city diplomacy runs in parallel with classical traditional state diplomacy as a subset of the "paradiplomacy" (Aldecoa and Keating, 1999; Tavares, 2016), a sub-state or subnational diplomacy (Criekemans, 2010), or municipal foreign policy (Leffel, 2018). In this regard, Rogier Van der Pluijm and Jan Melissen (2007, pp. 12–13) have described the aims cities wishing to deploy "diplomacy" as two-pronged: on the one hand, cities' diplomatic activities infringe upon the role of central governments, thereby often creating an adversarial relationship between cities and state actors (i.e., ministries of foreign affairs), similarly to how NGOs or corporate lobbies have carved a niche for themselves in the past; on the other hand, they are also tackling issues traditionally ignored by states, such as local infrastructure needs or bottom-up approaches to peacekeeping. This, of course, implies thinking, principally, of cities as political communities and thus as "polities" (Acuto et al., 2016, p. 10). Cities are increasingly recognized for their influence on global agendas and international processes. This isn't just a theoretical trend; cities demonstrate the value of their networking efforts (Karvounis, 2023). For example, the Climate Action in Megacities report (2015) from the C40 group shows that while state-led climate action is stagnant, 30% of the 10,000 climate actions by C40 Cities since COP 15 in Copenhagen succeeded due to city collaboration. C40, since its 2005 inception, facilitated four-fifths of this collaboration, leveraging over $2.8 billion in funding and impacting millions of urban dwellers worldwide (Acuto et al., 2016, p. 10). City diplomacy is thus a political process where cities establish and nurture formal and informal relationships with each other, complementing traditional state diplomacy. Cities promote their interests within international and national legal frameworks, aiming to influence other actors and organizations. They serve as solution-oriented entities for local, regional, national, or global issues. This definition emphasizes cities' active political role, participating in setting clear positions, pursuing specific interests, addressing common issues, and influencing the international agenda. In other words, cities are not passive entities subject to top-down logics (Le Galès, 2002, p. 262).

2.3   The Drivers of City Diplomacy

Although we lack definite studies to test the relevance and validity of their intercorrelation, the key drivers of city diplomacy are as such (Marchetti, 2021, pp. 63–67):

- *Mayor's attitude*: The personal determination of the mayor is crucial for a municipality to start cultivating relations with foreign counterparts. It is precisely the fact that city diplomacy is less institutionalized than state diplomacy that gives greater weight to the personal attitudes of city diplomats, such as mayors. Especially for smaller municipalities which often do not have a professional apparatus for city diplomacy, personal contacts between mayors and their foreign peers or other people are the main vehicle of the city's international diplomatic activities.
- *Citizens' pressure*: City diplomacy can also originate from the bottom-up pressure of citizens' activism, as in the case of nuclear-free cities.

- *Urban society*: International diasporas, tourists, businesses, religious communities, international experts, and diplomats are among the actors who can indirectly motivate a city to engage more in international activities.
- *Political culture*: When a political culture spreads among citizens and political elites, such that they are ripe for extracting the benefits of transnational politics, city diplomacy is likely to take place.
- *Historical track record*: The historical track record of past international activism by the city generates a sort of path dependency that may lead to more diplomatic actions.
- *Expediency*: City diplomacy might simply be an instrument to better serve city interests. Amsterdam is active in Ghana, Surinam, and Turkey because they are countries of origins of its migrants.
- *Resources*: Tangible resources linked to finance (e.g., EU programs), human resources, and bureaucratic assets are crucial for city diplomacy.
- *Type of economy*: If the city is either locally deprived of essential resources or has a significant export-oriented business community, city diplomacy is more likely to search for international ties to support the international projection of its local economic actors.
- *Institutional framework and degree of decentralization*: The autonomy of a city in foreign policy is also determined by the degree of freedom and decentralization allowed by the central state. The legal framework is often silent on this issue, the political dialogue between the central government and the cities is fundamental (see Chapter 4). The degree of decentralization and territorial devolution of power implies more or less autonomy for cities of course. In countries, such as Canada and the Netherlands with strong cultures of devolution, city diplomacy is a widespread practice.
- *Lack of national diplomacy*: City diplomacy may also serve as a functional substitute for "national" diplomacy when a territory aspires to sovereign independence, but still lacks official international recognition: this is the case in Palestinian cities for Palestine and Barcelona for Catalonia.
- *Geographical factors*: Cities close to borders, harbors, or rivers usually develop a more open mindset and a deeper inclination to reach out and connect to the world (see Rotterdam in the Netherlands, Shanghai in China, or Trieste in Italy).

2.4   The Goals of City Diplomacy

Local governments have plenty of tasks to fulfill for their own citizens. Why do they, on top of that, also want to get involved in city diplomacy? There are several reasons for this. As seen above, Van der Pluijm and Melissen (2007) identify six dimensions of city diplomacy: security, development, economy, culture, networks, and representation. However, these dimensions are misleading as they are not based on clear classification criterion, not distinguishing dimensions of city diplomacy from its forms. For Grandi (2020, p. 9), city diplomacy's goals can be divided into four groups: prevention of conflicts and reconciliation; development aid and solidarity; cooperation in addressing global challenges, such as climate change, migrations, gender equity, violent extremism, and urbanization; regional integration and solidarity. Marchetti (2021, pp. 61–62) considers that cities go global for pragmatic reasons, that is, find solutions that cannot be achieved with local action only; for personal and political ambitions; for idealism that produces offers of solidarity; and for activism which can push toward engagement on certain issue. We can thus identify five main goals: security, development, economy, culture, and political affairs (Surmacz, 2018). In reality many of the diplomatic activities undertaken by cities fall within more than one goal of city diplomacy.

Cities now engage in international security issues, emphasizing conflict prevention and peace efforts. City diplomacy often expresses solidarity, providing aid during crises. Local governments aim to protect global citizens, promoting peace. Initiatives, such as "Cities for Peace", pushed for resolutions against the Iraq war, with limited impact. "Mayors for Peace" advocates nuclear disarmament, involving thousands of cities but with modest diplomatic success (Surmacz, 2018, p. 13).

City authorities play a crucial role in addressing non-military security issues related to ecological and social threats. Cities are responsible for 70% of carbon dioxide emissions and are most affected by climate change. Despite challenges in international agreements, cities are actively addressing these issues, exemplified by the quote "While nations talk, cities act" from Michael Bloomberg, former Mayor of New York City. City initiatives against climate change often have a networked character, with global collaboration facilitated by organizations, such as United Cities and Local Governments (UCLG), World Association of the Major Metropolises (METROPOLIS), C40 Cities Climate Leadership Group (C40), and the World Mayors Council on Climate Change. This collaborative effort aims to achieve ambitious climate agreements and recognize the crucial role of local communities in climate protection.

City diplomacy isn't solely driven by solidarity and global challenges; self-interest is a factor too. Economic interests, such as trade connections, often initiate city diplomacy. Local governments seek gains from these programs, with economic goals being a significant focus. The economic dimension involves using foreign affairs competencies to enhance cities' competitiveness in the global economy (Grandi, 2020, p. 83). In this respect, cities compete against each other for an inflow of investments, tourists, location of large companies, or a chance to host prestigious cultural or sports events. Culture is an important part of diplomacy of every state and is also a significant element of city diplomacy (see Chapter 7). It is frequently a resource on the basis of which cities build their international position and a platform on which an international cooperation network is created (Grandi, 2020, p. 123). True, cities engage in lobbying, hold negotiations with corporations and international organizations, and build the city brand on the international arena. A special case of the economic dimension of city diplomacy is competition for hosting the Olympic Games (see Chapter 7). Cities actively engage in lobbying, negotiate with corporations and international organizations, and cultivate their international brand. The economic aspect includes competing to host events, such as the Olympic Games, involving diplomatic efforts with states, cities, and private actors. City authorities play a key role in creating strong coalitions for negotiations, participating in a "hard" diplomatic game (Acuto, 2013). In this sense, motivations for city diplomacy are often solution-oriented and pragmatic, addressing concrete issues. Some mayors aspire to lead innovative international actions, enhancing their municipality's performance, reputation, and economic growth through soft cultural promotion. Global involvement facilitates learning about fresh and innovative ideas (Johnson and Thomas, 2007, pp. 39–48; Van Ewijk and Baud, 2009, pp. 218–226; Wilson and Johnson, 2007, pp. 253–269) to attract investment and increase economic activity and to position the city's brand and identity on the global scene (Huggins, 2015, pp. 129–215).

Sometimes city diplomacy is also grounded in political reasons. And contrary to those scholars who argue that the decision of cities to go global is free of political considerations (Pipa and Bouchet, 2020, p. 603), we consider that power and prestige can motivate elected representatives to go global to gain visibility or even win elections. Furthermore, at the end of the 1980s, Western cities got involved in partner cooperation with Revolutionary People's Army (RPA) cities to express their solidarity in the fight against apartheid. Political reasons can also lead to a breach or suspension of partner cooperation. The authorities of Prague took a decision on suspending cooperation with Moscow and Petersburg in connection with Russia's aggression against Ukraine (Surmacz, 2018, p. 14).

2.5 The Actors of City Diplomacy

Without doubt, the most important role in city diplomacy is performed by their leaders, that is mayors (Surmacz, 2018, p. 15). They are the "ambassadors" of their cities on the international arena. Rudolph Giuliani, Michael Bloomberg and Bill de Blasio – former Mayors of New York City, Rahm Emanuel – former Mayor of Chicago, Boris Johnson – former Mayor of London, Yury Luzhkov – former Mayor of Moscow, or Eduardo Paes – former Mayor of Rio de Janeiro – these figures are recognizable also in the world politics. Big city mayors, increasingly influential, often ascend to national leadership roles. They actively engage in international affairs, participating in conferences, media, and hosting global summits. Criticizing states for global problem-solving inefficiencies, they establish international networks and propose solutions. The Global Parliament of Mayors, initiated by Benjamin Barber in 2016, stands out. Mayors worldwide join to address major challenges from the perspective of large cities, gaining significant political importance on the global stage.

Apart from the elected representatives, city diplomacy rests on the practitioners as well. The majority of local authorities have in their structures the units responsible for its management (Surmacz, 2018, p. 15). These units, in the form of offices or departments, usually situated at the offices of mayors, are accountable for planning and development of the city's "foreign policy", international economic missions, attraction of foreign investments, cooperation with partners, cultural exchange, the city's participation in international programs, but also, especially in the case of capital cities, relations with the diplomatic corps, international institutions, and NGOs.

Yet, the main actors in city diplomacy cannot be restricted to elected representatives or the practitioners (Marchetti, 2021, p. 60). The focus of the international engagement of municipalities is twofold. On the one hand, city governance is driven by the logic of efficiency and effectiveness, so local governments appear financially viable and citizen-oriented. On the other hand, city governance is underpinned by the democratic ideal of citizen empowerment. Both logics support the international activities of local authorities that require the active participation of a wider circle of actors (Marchetti, 2021, p. 60): (a) Citizens, civil society organizations, such as NGOs, think tanks, and ethnic groups; (b) economic and business organizations, such as chambers of commerce and private companies; and (c) educational and cultural bodies, such as schools, universities, research centers, museums, and theaters, can take active roles in the various forms of city diplomacy. Given the shortages of personnel for their international activities, cities could exploit the potential of local capital. Cities are typically skilled at forming alliances and collaborations with local and international, public and private groups. In this respect, given that partnership networks are a valuable resource for cities, it is vital for the municipal offices of international affairs to manage this resource more strategically and develop alliances, not only with other cities, but also with non-city players, such as NGOs, researchers, and corporations (Wang and Amiri, 2019).

2.6   The Tools of City Diplomacy

City diplomacy tools vary. Legal frameworks provide for partnerships through agreements. These aren't legally binding globally, making cities not globally accountable. However, strong local government commitment can yield tangible outcomes for stakeholders and communities. In this respect, the panorama of city diplomacy tools includes bilateral agreements, city networks, bilateral and multilateral projects, international events, and advocacy (Grandi, 2020).

2.6.1   Bilateral Agreements

Traditional bilateral agreements, such as town-twinnings (see Chapter 5), began to emerge in the middle of the 20th century as a method of organized municipal collaboration. A legal agreement is drafted to indicate the unique relationship between two cities based on cooperation agreements (CAs),[1] protocols of intent or Memorandum of Understanding (MoU),[2] between the two cities. Initially promoting friendship and cross-cultural exchange, bilateral agreements have evolved to prioritize trade and economic growth. These agreements open doors to new markets, products, exchanges in sports, art, education, culture, technology transfer, and development assistance. Completed partnerships involve institutional visits, direct ties with municipal offices, and citizen/student delegation exchanges. Town-twinning committees often run by locals with municipal support, enhance resident involvement through visits, exchange programs, and cultural events (Hubbard and Bell, 2013). While maintaining symbolic friendship, these nonbinding agreements are rarely canceled, preserving cities' legal existence amid shifting international objectives. Notably, bilateral agreements are undergoing significant changes, increasingly incorporating or strengthening economic elements (Grandi, 2020, p. 12).

2.6.2   City Networks

On the other hand, multilateral partnerships include thematic/geographical/project-based city networks (see Chapter 6), ceremonial alliances (e.g., Olympic cities, European and African Capitals of Culture), and European Groupings of Territorial Cooperation-EGTC (see Chapter 4).

2.6.3   Bilateral and Multilateral Projects

Bilateral and multilateral projects are short to middle-term international projects where municipalities engage with one or more foreign partners to "harness city diplomacy's potential to impact the city positively" (Grandi, 2020, p. 16). Such projects often focus on creating new partnerships (i.e. project-bound city networks) and introducing innovative solutions by exchanging best practices, introducing new technologies and initiating pilot projects. Unlike bilateral and multilateral agreements, these projects are set within a shorter and more specific timeframe, with goals that address the needs of the cities involved (Grandi, 2020).

2.6.4   International Events and International Advocacy

International events can be recurring, hosted by specific cities (e.g., the Cannes and Venice film festivals or the Cape Town Cycle Tour) or itinerant (e.g., the Olympic Games or the FIFA World Cup). These events provide opportunities for cities to boost their international profile (see Chapter 7) and their local economies in the short and (ideally) long term (Grandi, 2020). Cities often engage in international advocacy through city networks and advocacy campaigns related to, for example, human rights or climate change, which are not always aligned to the will and action of their national government (ibid.).

2.7   Conclusions

The growing importance of city diplomacy has long been discussed in the fields of urban studies and, to a lesser extent, international relations; nevertheless, these ideas have not been supported by much comprehensive empirical data up to this point. Although the idea of "city diplomacy" is not new, cities are becoming more important in international diplomacy using networks, such as International Council for Local Environmental Initiatives (ICLEI), Eurocities, and C40 to create platforms to participate in the multilayered and multi-sectored diplomatic environment. Issues, such as climate change and resilience become significant focal points of national diplomatic strategy and they are turning into the centers of attention for local action. In response to these shifts in national diplomacy, city diplomacy is also evolving. And in a post-pandemic world, new forms of city diplomacy will be the key in driving urban sustainability.

Notes

1 Cooperation Agreement (CA) outlines the cooperative terms of two entities to work in partnership on certain listed projects (Tavares, 2016, p. 64). Cooperation (or friendship) agreements represent weaker forms of cooperation, usually more specific in the content, with less formal protocols surrounding the adoption and usually a term, at which the agreement or memorandum may or may not renew automatically (Grandi, 2020, p. 11).

2 An even weaker for city partnership is represented by the Memorandum of Understanding (MoU). The MoU usually defines the partnership in more open, less precise terms than a town-twinning agreement or CA and is generally the only form of partnership that does not require a formal vote by the city council. As such, it is usually intended as a first step in a city-to-city partnership aiming at the signature of a town-twinning agreement or CA (Grandi, 2020, p. 11). Protocol of Intent or Letter of Intent or Memorandum of Understanding (MoU) is a document that expresses mutual accord on an issue between two or more parties. To be legally operative, an MoU must (1) identify the contracting parties; (2) spell out the subject matter of the agreement and its objectives; (3) summarize the essential terms of the agreement; and (4) must be signed by the contracting parties (Tavares, 2016, p. 65).

References

Acuto, M. (2013) "World Politics by Other Means? London, City Diplomacy and the Olympics", *The Hague Journal of Diplomacy* 8 (3–4), pp. 287–311. https://doi.org/10.1163/1871191X-12341255

Acuto, M., Morissette, M., Chan, D., and Leffel, B. (2016) *City Diplomacy and Twinning: Lessons from the UK, China and Globally*, Government Office for Science.

Acuto, M., and Rayner, S. (2016) "City Networks: Breaking Gridlocks or Forging (New) Lock-ins?", *International Affairs*, 92 (5), pp. 1147–1166.

Aldecoa, F., and Keating, M. (1999) "Introduction". In A. Aldecoa and M. Keating (Eds.) *Paradiplomacy in Action. The Foreign Relations of Subnational Governments* (pp. vii–x). London: Frank Cass Publishers.

Bush, K. (2003) *Building Capacity for Peace and Unity. The Role of Local Governments in Peacebuilding*, Ottawa: Federation of Canadian Municipalities.

Criekemans, D. (2010) "Regional Sub-State Diplomacy from a Comparative Perspective: Quebec, Scotland, Bavaria, Catalonia, Wallonia and Flanders", *The Hague Journal of Diplomacy*, 5 (1–2), pp. 37–64.

Curtis, S., and Acuto, M. (2018) "The Foreign Policy of Cities", *RUSI Journal*, 163 (6), pp. 8–17.

Grandi, L.K. (2020) *City Diplomacy*, Cham: Palgrave Macmillan.

Hocking, B.. (1993) *Localising Foreign Policy*, Basingstoke: Palgrave Macmillan.

Hubbard, J.M., and Bell, D. (2013) "Twin Cities: Territorial and Relational Geographies of 'Wordly' Manchester", *Urban Studies*, 50 (2), pp. 239–514.

Huggins, C. (2015) *"Local government transnational networking in Europe: a study of 14 local authorities in England and France"*, *PhD Thesis*, Portsmouth: University of Portsmouth.

Johnson, H., and Thomas, A. (2007) "Individual Learning and Building Organisational Capacity for Development", *Public Administration and Development*, 26 (1), pp. 39–48.

Karvounis, A. (2022) "City Diplomacy and Public Policy in the Era of COVID-19: Networked Responses from the Greek Capital", *Journal of Public Policy Studies*, 9 (2), pp. 47–62.

Karvounis, A. (2023) *City Diplomacy and the Europeanisation of Local Government. The Prospects of Networking in the Greek Municipalities*, Cham: Palgrave Macmillan.

La Porte, T. (2011) *City Diplomacy in the EU: A Framework of Analysis*, Pamplona: Universidad de Navarra.

Leffel, B. (2018) "Animus of the Underling: Theorising City Diplomacy in a World Society", *Hague Journal of Diplomacy*, 13 (4), pp. 502–522.

Le Galès, R. (2002) *European Cities: Social Conflicts and Governance*, Oxford: Oxford University Press.

Marchetti, R. (2021) *City Diplomacy. From City-States to Global Cities*, Ann Arbor: University Michigan Press.

Pipa, A.F., and Bouchet, M. (2020) "Multilateralism Restored? City Diplomacy in the COVID-19 Era", *Hague Journal of Diplomacy*, 15 (4), pp. 599–610.

Sizoo, A. (2007) "City Diplomacy", *Concept Paper*, Hague: VNG.

Soldatos, P. (1990) "An Explanatory Framework for the Study of Federated States as Foreign Policy Actors". In H. Michelmann and P. Soldatos (Eds.) *Federalism and International Relations. The Role of Subnational Units* (pp. 34–53). Oxford: Clarendon Press.

Surmacz, B. (2018) "City Diplomacy", *Barometr Regionalny*, 16 (1), pp. 7–18.

Tavares, R. (2016) *Paradiplomacy: Cities and States as Global Players*, New York: Oxford University Press.

Van der Pluijm, R., and Melissen, J. (2007) *City Diplomacy: The Expanding Role of Cities in International Politics*, Clingendael: Netherlands Institute of International Relations.

Van Ewijk, E., and Baud, I.S.A. (2009) "Partnerships between Dutch Municipalities and Municipalities in Countries of Migration to the Netherlands; Knowledge Exchange and Mutuality", *Habitat International*, 33 (2), pp. 218–226.

Wang, J., and Amiri, S. (2019) *Building a Robust Capacity Framework for U.S. City Diplomacy*, Los Angeles: USC Centre on Public Diplomacy.

Wilson, G., and Johnson, H. (2007) "Knowledge, Learning and Practice in North–South Practitioner-Practitioner Municipal Partnerships", *Local Government Studies*, 33 (2), pp. 253–269.

Reports and Official Publications

Committee of the Regions (2009) "City Diplomacy", *Resolution*, 78th Plenary Session, 12–13 February, Brussels: CoR.

Congress of Local and Regional Authorities (2008) "City Diplomacy", *Recommendation*, 234, Strasbourg: Council of Europe.

VNG (2008) *The Hague Agenda on City Diplomacy*, Hague: Association of Netherlands Municipalities.

3 The Forerunners of City Diplomacy

3.1 Introduction

The evolution of international relations and local administration has given rise to modern city diplomacy, with cities playing an increasingly significant role in global affairs over the past century. Historically, cities have interacted for growth, driven by economic and demographic expansion within loose forms of centralization. Notable instances include the Hanseatic League during the Middle Ages, a cross-border governance of almost 200 cities that lasted for five centuries, serving as a precursor to modern city networks. While the Peace of Westphalia in 1648 established states as the sole players in international relations, the inception of contemporary city diplomacy is often traced back to the 1913 International Congress on the Art of Building Cities and Organizing Community Life. A few years later (1928), the first worldwide city network, the International Union of Cities (later IULA), was founded and played a crucial role in empowering cities for post-war reconciliation, whereas town-twinnings expanded in Western Europe, addressing past grievances. Since then, city networks, the most influential type of international partnerships of local authorities, multiplied, reaching over 120 today. United Cities and Local Governments (UCLG), the largest and most representative worldwide city network, Eurocities, the most significant regional network in Europe, Metropolis and the Organization of Islamic Capitals and Cities (OICC) have facilitated international collaboration, connecting thousands of politicians, experts, and officials across the globe. This chapter introduces the historical trajectory of city diplomacy. It is divided into three sections arranged in chronological order. The first section considers the ancient roots of the modern city diplomacy till the advent of the nation-state. The second section provides us with historical knowledge on city diplomacy from the Peace of Westphalia till the modern era of city partnerships in the first quarter of the 20th century. The last section is focused on the contemporary period since the World War II. What unites all these periods is the idea that cities themselves are networks; there is no such thing as a single city. Cities need each other and the single city is an abstraction defining situations that cannot exist.

DOI: 10.4324/9781003470908-5

3.2   The Ancient Path of City Diplomacy

We usually tend to consider the Peace of Westphalia in 1648 as the beginning of modern international diplomacy (Marchetti, 2021, p. 3). Yet, the cradle of modern diplomacy is traced back to city-states and not countries. Greek city-states, such as Athína (Athens), Spárti (Sparta), Kórinthos (Corinth), Thíva (Thebes), Siracusa (Syracuse), Égina (Aegina), Ródos (Rhodes), Árgos, Erétria, and Elis, also known as poleis, were the separate communities of ancient Greece. Starting as just a few divided areas of land, the polis expanded into over 1,000 different cities. The concept of *polis*, however, is an ancient concept and reflects the ancient Greeks' understanding of their own political and social order, whereas the concept of *city-state* is a modern heuristic concept invented by historians to describe, not only the Hellenic poleis, but also a number of other city-state cultures ranging from the Mixtec city-states in Mexico to the Malay city-states in Indonesia and from the Viking city-states in Ireland to the Swahili city-states in Kenya and Tanzania. The Hellenic civilization from the Archaic period down to the Roman Empire is only one of many civilizations organized into urbanized micro-states rather than forming one or a few large macro-states, each dotted with cities (Hansen, 2000, 1996).

Greek city-states were characterized by their distinct governing laws, customs, and interests. Barrier walls surrounded these city-states to defend against external threats. Many featured a temple or acropolis on elevated terrain, offering a strategic vantage point. The formation of Greek city-states can be attributed to the physical features of the Mediterranean region, including islands and rugged terrain, which created distant population centers. Waterways facilitated travel between these locations (Hansen and Nielsen, 2004). Additionally, the Greek nobility played a role in maintaining city-state autonomy, resisting the establishment of a single, universal monarchy in favor of preserving individual city-state sovereignty.

Although the concept of city-states no longer exists, many of the former polis still operate as cities or towns throughout the Mediterranean today. Yet, well before Westphalia these cities acted as foreign policy entities (Kurbalija, 2021). Athens and other Greek city-states would send and receive envoys to one another to negotiate political and social issues. A proxenos (pl. proxenoi) was a Greek consular agent and a citizen of the city-state in which he resided. The classical proxenia, as attested in the entire Hellenic world, was a privilege and an honor bestowed by polis A on a citizen of polis B who thereby officially was assigned the task of furthering the interests of polis A in his own polis and, in particular, the task of hosting and helping citizens of polis A when they came as visitors. As envoys, proxenoi had a task of gathering information, but their primary responsibility was trade. Proxenoi were a type of early honorary consuls, ambassadors, and lobbyists. A proxenos would use whatever influence he had in his own city to promote policies, friendships, and alliances with the city he represented. He was expected to handle all high-level political matters, as well as to provide support and housing for visitors from the sending state (merchants, representatives, politicians). Proxenoi were granted certain immunities, such as asylum in case the sending state turned against him, or free and safe travel during both peace and war. The position of the proxenos held prestige and was hereditary. During the classical Greek period, it is probable that all well-known Athenian politicians held one or more positions as proxenoi (for example, Demosthenes was a proxenos in Athens for Thebes). A presbus (pl. presbeis) or envoy was a senior citizen involved in advocacy, similar to a public diplomat. Presbeis were great orators who went on unpaid, ad-hoc missions. Delegations of envoys were often big, numbering 20–30 people. They were prominent representatives of the sending states. In many cases, they used to address the citizens and senate of the receiving state, and tried to persuade the elite of the receiving state about the position of their country. A *keryx* (herald) was an inviolable Greek messenger. In Homer's time, the kēryx was simply a trusted attendant or retainer of a chieftain. The role of kerykes expanded to include: acting as inviolable messengers between states even in time of war; proclaiming meetings of a council, popular assembly, or a court of law; reciting the formulas of prayer in important meetings; and summoning persons to attend. They were regarded as the offspring of Hermes. Kerykes were general-purpose messengers and masters of ceremonies. The diplomatic responsibilities of the heralds were to serve as a "truce-bearer" prior to the start of the Panhellenic Games and to make announcements there. More important was their task of going ahead of ambassadors in order to secure guarantees for their safe reception. They were also responsible for issuing ultimatums and declarations of war. Heralds were the early masters of protocol (Hamilton, 1979; Kurbalija, 2021; Mosley, 1973).

Early multilateral diplomacy was developed around the idea of truce during the Olympic Games and other common festivities. At that time, the representatives of city-states used to gather here. It was also a moment when they shared a common identity, and a good opportunity to negotiate. The diplomatic innovation of Common Peace was born here and included the permanent peace between the Greek city-states. The idea of common peace can still be found today and was one of the founding principles of the League of Nations and our modern system which is based on the Charter of the United Nations. Multilateral diplomacy occurred to a greater extent in the states-system's religious leagues (neighboring communities sharing a deity) and large-member military alliances (or "leagues") established for defense and offense. One of the examples of the well-developed multilateral alliances is the Second Athenian Confederacy, a defensive alliance created in 378/7 BC. Its purpose was to guard against the growing fear that Sparta would not honor the common peace of the Greek cities. The famous Decree of Aristoteles described its purpose and defensive character, and invited others to join, including any "barbarians" (non-Greeks) on the mainland or islands. These were known as military alliances of ancient Greek poleis. They comprise the terms *symmachia* and *koinon*, both of which meant a league for the mutually supportive conduct of war, both offensive and defensive. Apart from the domination of large states, such as Athens and Sparta, the leagues were named after the ethnic regions they were intended to defend.[1]

In particular, "Amphictyony" or "Amphictyonic League" refers to an ancient religious association of tribes that existed in Archaic Greece before the rise of the Greek city-states. These associations were formed to establish connections between neighboring tribes and often revolved around the worship of a particular deity. One notable example is the Delphic Amphictyony, also known as the Great Amphictyonic League, which was organized to support the greater temples of Apollo and Demeter. This league had significant religious authority and was responsible for protecting and administering important religious sites. The council of the Delphic Amphictyony had the power to pronounce punishments against offenders and conduct sacred wars. Members of the league were obliged to pledge themselves by oath, and representatives from 12 founding populations convened at Thermopylae and Delphi. The Delphic Amphictyony was founded to protect and administer the temples of Apollo in Delphi and Demeter in Anthela, near Thermopylae. According to legend, it was founded by Amphictyon, the brother of Hellen, the common ancestor of all Hellenes. The league aimed to prevent the complete destruction of any member in war and to ensure the protection of water supplies, even during times of conflict. Over time, the Delphic Amphictyony admitted new members and expanded its influence, particularly after the defense of the sanctuary against the Gauls. However, its authority gradually declined, and it was eventually replaced by the Panhellenion established by the Roman emperor Hadrian in the 2nd-century CE. Despite its decline, the Delphic Amphictyony played a significant role in ancient Greek religious and political life, serving as a forum for collective decision-making and religious governance (Jeffery, 1978). These leagues were an intermediate step between the independent poleis and the Macedonian, Roman, or Persian provincial administrations that brought the poleis to an end and replaced the politeia with a local government subordinate to a province. "Federation", "confederacy", and a third term, "sympoliteia", only describe the degree of independence or lack of it. Apart from Greek city-states and their alliances, Ancient Egyptian city-states (Thebes or Memphis), the large pre-Columbian Mesoamerican cities (Chichen Itza, Tikal, Monte Alban, or Tenochtitlan), the central Asian cities along the Silk Road or the Viking colonial cities in medieval Ireland, history is pregnant with examples of cities that had contacts with foreign lands in a world of difficult communication and mobility (Tavares, 2016, p. 10).

3.3   The Medieval Path of City Diplomacy

Janet Abu-Lughod's (1989) study of the medieval Eurasian ecumene in the 13th and 14th centuries focuses on cities rather than countries. Described as an archipelago of towns, it examines a network of cities forming a system in formation (Gills, 2014). The system includes Europe, the Eastern Mediterranean, the Persian Gulf, western Indian Ocean, eastern Indian Ocean and Southeast Asia, and China, with major trading centers as key empirical focuses. The archipelago consists of eight interlinked subsystems, grouped into three larger circuits – western European, Middle Eastern, and Far Eastern. Unlike the modern world-system, there's no overarching hierarchy; coexisting core powers replace a hegemonic power. The archipelago is less interdependent, with two east-west routes connecting major cities. However, Abu-Lughod's analysis has gaps, omitting circuits, such as the Baltic, Baltic/Dnieper-Volga/Black & Caspian Seas, West African-trans-Saharan-Mediterranean, Indian Ocean (including Kilwa, Sofala, and Mauritius), and East/Southeast Asia (excluding the Korean peninsula and Japan), limiting the completeness of the "Afro-Eurasian world system" in the medieval period.

In contrast, within Europe during that time, there existed a network of cities, particularly institutionalized in the northern pole of cities, with Bruges as a prominent representative. This network extended beyond a single city and was politically organized, pre-dating the rise of the modern world-system. Notably, the Hanseatic League stands out as one of the most well-known historical organizations of cities functioning as a network. Initially formed by long-distance merchants, it evolved into a formidable association of cities: the Hanseatic League.

According to Dollinger (1970, p. 166), the formation of the city network was clearly the work of the merchants. True, the geographical outcome of the trading activity from the northern pole (Bruge), across North Sea (London), to the far north (Bergen) and Eastern Europe (Novgorod) resulted in a cohesive city network. In addition, German Hanse was connected to Mediterranean city networks from Cologne through Frankfurt and Nuremberg to Milan and Genoa and Venice. The standard way in which city linkages were created and maintained was by merchant partnerships. It is not surprising thus that the cradle of modern diplomacy can be traced back to Northern Italy in the 14th century and spread to the rest of Western and Northern Europe in the following hundred years. Milan played a leading role, especially under Francesco Sforza, a 15th-century *condottiero*, who established permanent embassies in the other city states of Northern Italy (Tavares, 2016, p. 10). In fact, during Renaissance, major cities, such as Venice and Florence had diplomatic networks that included permanent missions abroad. Several other cities across Europe and Asia have a long tradition of exercising political, commercial, cultural, religious, and military power on a vast territorial scale, including Rome, Genoa, Cairo, Constantinople, and Baghdad and Chengdu in China. Despite such a relevant role played by cities throughout the centuries, the founding moment of the current international order, the 1648 Peace of Westphalia, clearly stated that international relations are the exclusive realm of states. With the modern age and the Westphalian order, cities were marginalized by the rising nation-states and their bureaucracies that encompassed diplomatic activities (Grandi, 2020, p. 39; Marchetti, 2021, p. 49).

3.4 The Modern Path of City Diplomacy

According to Tavares (2016, p. 11), the first modern attempts at fostering international exchanges of local governments were born in the late 19th century when crown colonies under British rule appointed their agent-generals to either London or Paris. In the early 20th century, the first modern generation of city diplomacy was based on formalized bilateral relationships (in many cases opportunistic or idiosyncratic in nature) that were mainly centered on cultural, economic, or humanitarian purposes. This is the period of "sister city" relationships – or what has become known as "town-twinnings" (Kosovac et al., 2020).

Established as the first international cities organization, the International Union of Local Authorities (IULA), also known as the Union Internationale des Villes (UIV), originated in 1913 during the World Exhibition in Ghent, Belgium, and aimed to foster common ideas among cities. Despite two closures during the early 20th century due to wars, IULA persisted in its goals. In 2003, it merged with the United Towns Organisation (UTO) to form the new world organization, UCLG. Operating since 1 January 2004, with headquarters in Barcelona, Spain, UCLG continues to advocate for local governments, representing their interests globally, including engagements with the United Nations and other international agencies (Balbim, 2016, p. 140).

After the end of the war, several European cities, emerging from the devastation, actively engaged in peace and reconciliation efforts through the establishment of town-twinning agreements. These initiatives, which involved activities, such as cultural exchange, diaspora relations, and commercial market development, were often driven by the aspirations of political leaders, city governments, or stakeholders. Despite their varied nature, these early relationships laid the groundwork for more systematic, coherent, and institutionalized city-diplomacy efforts (Kosovac et al., 2020, p. 6). The Council of European Municipalities (CEMR) played a pivotal role in this development, being founded in 1951, with offices in several European countries. In its inaugural gathering, 50 mayors from across Europe negotiated twinning agreements and established standards. Concurrently, President Dwight D. Eisenhower introduced new strategies, including the establishment of programs, such as Sister Cities International in 1956 (Acuto et al., 2021; Tavares, 2016, p. 13). This era of city diplomacy witnessed municipalities and metropolitan governments collaborating on idea exchange and business facilitation, evolving into a complex system of transnational communities of practice. City networks also emerged during this period, serving as forums for collective action and advocacy bodies to ensure urban and local voices, were heard by higher levels of government and international interests. This model drew inspiration from historical precedents, such as the Hanseatic League and had been tested in the early days of modern multilateralism, as seen in the case of IULA. In 1955, city diplomacy took on a new level of organization when

Giorgio La Pira, the mayor of Florence, invited mayors from capital cities worldwide to discuss the potential role of cities in building peace. Despite the Cold War political climate, the conference drew mayors from the US, USSR, and even the People's Republic of China, which Western governments had not yet recognized. This marked a significant moment in the formalization and internationalization of city diplomacy efforts (Balbim, 2016, p. 141).

Following the Florence initiative, various international associations of cities began to emerge globally. In 1985, the Metropolis network was established, currently comprising 154 representatives and being one of the significant networks associated with the UCLG. City networks served as platforms, not only for exchanging ideas and facilitating commerce, but also for collective action on policy issues (Acuto et al., 2021, p. 140). These coalitions advocated for local interests in the global policy arena, marking cities' entry onto the global stage and forming "new types of global politics of place" (Sassen, 2017, p. 149), basically, thanks to their networks, perhaps the oldest, most visible and vocal form of city diplomacy. As Bouteligier (2013, p. 2) has put it, cities, through networks, are both spaces of innovation and places of leadership. Cities, recognizing a "governance gap", turned to each other to systematically channel shared interests and goals, increasing their international influence through "soft forms of governance". Rather than merely seeking a seat at the global table, cities aimed to directly influence and shape global agendas, utilizing city networks as effective channels to promote their political interests (Atkinson and Rossignolo, 2010).

The late years of the Cold War and the early 1990s witnessed a mix of the "first generation" forms of city diplomacy, such as Mayors for Peace (founded in 1982), a global campaign of cities to promote disarmament (Acuto et al., 2021, p. 140; Kosovac et al., 2020, p. 6). Novel forms of city networking engagements also emerged, including the International Council for Local Environment Initiatives (ICLEI) in 1990. ICLEI not only involved city-to-city exchange, but also featured explicitly institutionalized secretariats, facilitating policy mobility and resource and knowledge exchange among cities. Concurrently, several UN organizations, such as UNESCO, UN-Habitat, and the World Health Organization, initiated numerous programs, supporting the evolution of city diplomacy from symbolic twinning to a more practical diplomatic activity, involving thousands of local governments globally (Acuto et al., 2021, p. 140; Kosovac et al., 2020, p. 6).

In the 1990s, there was a remarkable growth in multilateral subnational arrangements globally, particularly in the environmental domain. This surge of interest in cities was ignited by various policy changes and initiatives, including the Council of Europe's affirmation of the local autonomy principle (see Chapter 4), the formalization of social and economic cohesion as a responsibility of European institutions, the promotion of structural and cohesion funds, and the establishment of the Committee of the Regions (CoR) in 1994. This period witnessed a significant proliferation of diverse networks, reflecting an extensive and impactful development (Fernández de Losada, 2019, p. 20). As Acuto (2020, p. viii) argues, city networks may have begun to take on a more active role in international politics, acting less as expansive coalitions of sister cities, such as those of the 1990s, and more as secretariats of international nongovernmental organizations (NGOs), coordinating intricate partnerships of cities, private sector players, states, and multilaterals. UCLG, Organization of Islamic Capitals and Cities, Med Cities, C40-Cities Climate Leadership Group, ICLEI, U20 Mayors Summit, Union for the Mediterranean (ARLEM), Eastern Partnership (CORLEAP), Mayors for Peace, and Eurocities constitute some of the most effective urban multilateral tools for local authorities to navigate global politics. As Sassen has pointed out, whether they are large, "global" or small cities, their international influence becomes even greater in the context of city networks (Sassen, 1991, 2002).

At the turn of the century, cities assumed more significant global responsibilities, aligning with major global priorities (Taylor, 2004). The institutionalization of municipalism gained traction, elevating its exposure and recognition globally. The formation of UCLG in 2004 marked a pivotal moment (UCLG, 2013). This led to heightened attention to urban and territorial issues in global agendas, exemplified by SDG 11 in the 2030 Agenda and the New Urban Agenda. Notable achievements followed, including the recognition of local and regional authorities as a Major Group by the UN's Economic and Social Committee (ECOSOC) and the establishment of the Global Taskforce of Local and Regional Governments (GTF) to coordinate the voices of local governments in global political processes (Fernández de Losada, 2019, p. 21).

3.5   Conclusions

History is pregnant with examples of cities that had contacts with foreign lands: from Greek city-states to the current multilateral partnerships of local authorities. Although cities have always maintained international relations, the concept of city diplomacy is relatively new. As a matter of fact, the way in which the various activities, often referred to as city diplomacy, are pursued have changed substantially. Up until 1990s, cities' partnerships were mostly bilateral agreements (see town-twinnings). Since then, one overarching change has been the general shift from bilateral toward multilateral relations, alongside the growing ambition to strengthen the voice in multilateral affairs. However networked and interdependent cities may become in terms of their economic, technocratic, and cultural functions, they live under the law and in the shadow of the legal jurisdiction and executive and fiscal authority of states that are still very powerful. In this respect, the relationship between the national governments and local authorities does matter for determining what a city can or cannot do beyond national borders. The next chapter delves into the legal standing of cities in their international partnerships.

Note

1 See Aeolian or Aiolian Dodecapolis, Ionian League, Galatian League, Chrysao-
rian League, Lycian League, Macedonian League, Chalcidian League, Thessalian
League, Aenianian League, Oetean League, Leahue of Magnetes, Boeotian League,
Phocial League, Amphictyonic League, Euboean League, Delian League, League
of Islanders, League of Corinth, Achaean League, Peloponnesian League, League
of Free Laconians, Arcadian League, Cretan League, Epirote League, Acarnanian
League, Aetolian League, Koinon of the Zagorisians (Hatzopoulos, 2004).

References

Abu-Lughod, J.L. (1989) *Before European Hegemony. The World System A.D. 1250–1350*,
New York: Oxford.

Acuto, M. (2020) "Prologue: A New Generation of City Diplomacy". In S. Amiri and
E. Sevin (Eds.) *City Diplomacy. Current Trends and Future Prospects* (pp. vii–xi).
Basingstoke: Palgrave Macmillan.

Acuto, M., Hartley, K., and Kosovac, A. (2021) "City Diplomacy: Another Generational Shift?", *Diplomatica*, 3 (1), pp. 137–146.

Atkinson, R., and Rossignolo, C. (2010) "Cities and the 'soft side' of Europeanisa-
tion: The Role of Urban Networks". In A. Hamedinger and A. Wolffhardt (Eds.)
The Europeanisation of Cities, Urban Change and Urban Networks (pp. 197–225).
Amsterdam: Techne Press.

Balbim, R. (2016) "City Diplomacy: Global Agendas, Local Agreements". In R.
Balbim (Ed.) *The Geopolitics of Cities. Old Challenges, New Issues* (pp. 123–170).
Brasilia: IPEA.

Bouteligier, S. (2013) *Cities, Networks, and Global Environmental Governance. Spaces
of Innovation, Places of Leadership*, New York and London: Routledge.

Dollinger, P. (1970) *The German Hansa*, London: Macmillan.

Fernández de Losada, A. (2019) "Towards a Cooperative Ecosystem of City Networks".
In A. Fernández de Losada and H. Abdullah (Eds.) *Rethinking the Ecosystem of International City Networks* (pp. 19–29). Barcelona: Cidob Edicions.

Gills, B.K. (2014) "Janet Abu-Lughod and the World System: The History of World
System Development and the Development of World System History", *Journal of
World Systems Research*, 20 (2), pp. 174–179.

Grandi, L.K. (2020) *City Diplomacy*, Cham: Palgrave Macmillan.

Hamilton, C.D. (1979) *Sparta's Bitter Victories: Politics and Diplomacy in the Corin-
thian War*, Ithaca and London: Cornell University Press..

Hansen, M.H. (1996) "ΠΟΛΛΑΧΩΣ ΠΟΛΙΣ ΛΕΓΕΤΑΙ (Arist. Pol. 1276a23): The
Copenhagen Inventory of Poleis and the Lex Hafniensis de Civitate", *CPCActs*, 3,
pp. 7–72.

Hansen, M.H. (2000) "Conclusion: The Impact of City-State Cultures on World
History". In M.H. Hansen (Ed.) *A Comparative Study of Thirty City-State Cultures*
(pp. 597–623). Copenhangen: The Royal Danish Academy of Science and Letters.

Hansen, M.H., and Nielsen, T.H. (2004) "Introduction". In M.H. Hansen and T.H.
Nielsen (Eds.) *An Inventory of Archaic and Classical Poleis*. Oxford: Oxford University Press.

Hatzopoulos, M.B. (2004) "*Makedonia*". In M.H. Hansen and T.H. Nielsen (Eds.) *An
Inventory of Archaic and Classical Poleis*. Oxford: Oxford University Press.

Jeffery, L.H. (1978) *Archaic Greece. The City-States c.700–500 B.C,* London: Methuen.

Kosovac, A., Hartley, K., Acuto, M., and Gunning, D. (2020) *Conducting City Diplomacy. A Survey of International Engagement in 47 Cities,* Chicago-Parkville: The Chicago Council on Global Affairs & Connected Cities Lab.

Kurbalija, J. (2021) "Ancient Greek diplomacy: Politics, new tools and negotiation, 'Diplomacy and Technology: A historical journey'", *DiploFoundation,* [Online], URL: https://www.diplomacy.edu/histories/ancient-greek-diplomacy-politics-new-tools-and-negotiation/.

Marchetti, R. (2021) *City Diplomacy. From City-States to Global Cities,* Ann Arbor: University Michigan Press.

Mosley, D.J. (1973). *Envoys and Diplomacy in Ancient Greece,* Stuttgart: Steiner.

Sassen, S. (2017) "Global Cities: Places for Researching the Translocal". In S. Hall and R. Burdett (Eds.) *The SAGE Handbook of the 21st Century City* (pp. 143–158). London: Sage.

Sassen, S. (2002) *Global Networks, Linked Cities,* New York: Routledge.

Tavares, R. (2016) *Paradiplomacy – Cities and States as Global Players,* New York: Oxford University Press.

Taylor, P.J. (2004) *World City Network. A Global Urban Analysis,* London and New York: Routledge.

UCLG (2013) "100 Years: Testimonies". *UCLG Official Website,* https://issuu.com/uclgcglu/docs/libro_centenario-web_1_

4 The Institutional Framework of City Diplomacy

4.1 Introduction

As known, local governments' international relations develop within the framework of the competences vested in them by the national laws. The applicable legal frameworks in the different countries are extremely diverse and often involve different levels or tiers, such as international conventions and treaties, national laws, regional and municipal regulations, etc. In addition to the many often overlapping legal frameworks, the scope of cities' transnational actions has also been subject to multiple, often obscure and contradictory legalistic interpretations. At the international law level, overall recognition of the legal status of cities is very limited. The Vienna Conventions on diplomatic and consular relations (in 1961 and 1963, respectively) have regulated and recognized the state as the only official actor in international relations. Despite that, the United Nations and the EU have endorsed the agenda of transforming relations between localities and their states, as demonstrated through efforts to promote an agenda of "decentralization" and "subsidiarity". The EU legal environment has only recently started to recognize cities' international role. As a matter of fact, the adoption of the Regulation on a European Grouping of Territorial Cooperation (EGTC) in 2006 was a "major change" in the legal framework for territorial cooperation because it was the first Community instrument with regulatory scope in the field, which brought cooperation between authorities located in different European states to the heart of the integration process, since, until then, there was no specific overarching legal framework instrument for transnational cooperation and the bulk of legal instruments for transnational European cooperation had been drawn in practice solely for cross-border cooperation in the institutional framework of the Council of Europe (CoE). In this respect, this chapter explores the international, European and national trends of the legal environment in which cities operate internationally.

4.2 The International Trends

Not much has been achieved in terms of rules and regulations at international level to recognize the new role played by local authorities.

DOI: 10.4324/9781003470908-6

Regardless of the particular country or legislation, local governments have no legal status in formal international public law. Traditionally, only national states have *ius tractatuum* as explicitly stated by Article 6 ("Every state possesses capacity to conclude treaties") and 2(a) ("'treaty' means an international agreement concluded between *States* in written form and governed by international law, whether embodied in a single instrument or in two or more related instruments and whatever its particular designation") of the 1969 Vienna Convention on the Law of Treaties. Cities are often in a legal vacuum. No treaties, UN conventions or International Court of Justice decisions mention or acknowledge the existence of local governments as entities directly subject to international law. In fact, as far as their legal status is concerned, local governments are subordinated to and represented by states. Besides, only states can be UN members. Since the mid-20th century states have recongnized the capacity of local governments to town-twining, but that is all. Actually, the failed experiment with the free cities, such as Krakow, Shanghai, Danzig and Fiume, as well as that of the internationalized cities and territories, such as Tangiers and Jerusalem, proved unsustainable and generated more problems (Marchetti, 2021, p. 58). Town-twinning, instead, has been approved as an exceptionally valuable mechanism for forging closer relations among peoples under several UN decisions – mainly Economic and Social Council Resolutions 1028 (XXXVII) and 1217 (XLII) and the General Assembly's Resolutions 2058 (XX) and 2861 (XXVI). In fact, the UN has brought about a normative transformation that might lead in the future to a new legal setting that accommodates cities' claims (Garesché, 2007).

In 1998, following Habitat II in Istanbul (1996), the UN Centre for Human Settlements and the World Association of Cities and Local Authorities Coordination drafted the text titled "Towards a World Charter of Local Self-Government", inspired by the European Charter of Local Self-Government (ECLSG) (see Section 4.3). Despite extensive debates among local authorities worldwide, supported by UN-Habitat, the World Charter has not been adopted. Instead, the UN General Assembly ratified the Istanbul Declaration and the Habitat 1996 Agenda to regulate relations with local governments. The Advisory Committee of Local Authorities (UNACLA), established in 2000, became the first local authority advisory body to the UN, with UNACLA acting as the formal interlocutor on local government-related issues. In 2002, the General Assembly reinforced the role of the UN Centre for Human Settlements, transforming it into UN-Habitat under the Economic and Social Council (ECOSOC). To ensure the legality of actions beyond national borders, a town council must be acquainted with the Istanbul Declaration, Habitat Agenda, ECOSOC, and General Assembly resolutions. While national laws need adaptation to support transnational actions by town councils, any local government can advocate for international relations based on these documents (Garesché, 2007, p. 45).

4.3 The European Trends

The dominant objective of cross-border cooperation in Europe after the Second World War was to strengthen political ties and maintain peace. Since the 1960s, the CoE has been a major promoter of cross-border cooperation as a means to help the diffusion of local democracy and good neighboring relations (Amilhat-Szary and Fourny, 2006; Bages Bechade, 2003; Bataillou, 2002; De Sousa, 2012, p. 9; Scott, 2006, 2012). Issues of culture, economy, and environment were integrated into cross-border cooperation actions (Malcolm and Bort, 1998, p. 67).

In 1980, the CoE introduced the "Madrid Convention", formally known as the Outline Convention on Transfrontier Co-operation between Territorial Communities or Authorities. This Convention established a legal framework for inter-state and local cooperation, recognizing the right of territorial communities to collaborate across national borders. It pioneered the concept of referring to national law for fulfilling transfrontier obligations and introduced the formation of transfrontier cooperation bodies. However, the nature and scope of cooperation were limited by the powers of local and regional authorities, leading to potential legal issues arising from diverse legal regimes governing European local and regional entities. Since 1981, the Madrid Convention has been signed by 41 countries and ratified by 39, supplemented by three additional protocols (1995, 1998, 2009). Despite these efforts, legal issues persisted, especially when states did not ratify the Third Protocol and governments had to sign mutual agreements to implement the Madrid Convention (Committee of the Regions, 2001).

The adoption of the ECLSG in 1985 resulted from CoE member states endorsing local democracy. ECLSG safeguards local authorities' rights and compels ratified governments to adhere to various requirements, principles, and practices. Above all, the Charter was an attempt to recognize the right of territorial communities to engage in transfrontier cooperation and provide a basis for a municipal foreign policy (Council of Europe, 1985a, Art. 10). In contrast to the functional considerations of paragraph 1, paragraph 2 is concerned with groups that typically work to represent all local governments of a specific kind or type at regional or national levels (Council of Europe, 1985b). Additionally, Article 10.2 acknowledges local governments' freedom to join international associations of local government (city networks included) to advance and protect their own interests and objectives on an international or worldwide scale (e.g., Council of European Municipalities and Regions (CEMR); United Cities and Local Governments (UCLG)). The right of local governments to cooperate is reiterated in paragraph 3, but it does so in a particular way: local governments in one country have the right to collaborate with their counterparts in another. This paragraph outlines the freedom to participate in transnational or transfrontier cooperation, which is another form of intermunicipal cooperation. Transfrontier cooperation can take many different forms, ranging from more or less symbolic town-twinnings between distant local authorities to extensive co-operation agreements between local authorities that are located on either side of an international border, share a common cultural heritage, protect a common natural resource, or desire to carry out projects of mutual interest (Council of Europe, 1980).

Since 2004, the European Commission and the Council of Europe, inspired by the Madrid Convention, initiated discussions on a tool for "trans-European" cooperation covering all local authority collaborations. Regulation (EC) No. 1082/2006, effective 5 July 2006, provided a legislative framework for cross-border, transnational, and inter-regional territorial cooperation (Committee of the Regions, 2007, p. 10). Building on the INTERREG initiative, it introduced significant changes, offering a legal personality under European Law for EGTCs, the first institutional framework for European cooperation. EGTCs, governed by conventions and statutes, have distinct features, including cross-border nature, extensive legal capacity, a single registered office, and the requirement for organs like an assembly and a director (Committee of the Regions, 2007, pp. 6–7; Soós, 2013, p. 522). As Papisca (2008) asserts, the EGTC "is the most advanced instrument on exercising territorial autonomy in the international system today": first, because it is a real supranational legal instrument, not based on an agreement among states; second, because within the "European Grouping", local governments have similar ranking to states; and finally, because local authorities from non-EU members can join the EGTC if there is nothing in their legislation that contradicts European legislation. We must emphasize the influence of this last point in non-EU areas: not merely to acknowledge the power of town halls but to promote consistency with the European legal framework and the principles on which it is based (La Porte, 2013). Article 3 of the EGTC Regulation mandates members to be national, regional, or local authorities or other public bodies. Notably, the Regulation revolutionized practices by allowing national governments to participate alongside local and regional governments, fostering multilevel governance and supporting territorial cohesion (Committee of the Regions, 2007, p. 10, 2018a, p. 7). EGTCs engage in diverse activities, contributing to ETC programs, Cohesion Policy projects, and various European, national, and regional initiatives (Jacob, 2013). They serve as multilevel governance instruments, fostering cross-border collaboration in public services, transportation, education, and planning roles in environmental protection, transport, tourism, and economic cooperation (Committee of the Regions, 2018b, p. 8). Since 2006, 89 EGTCs have been established, with 21 member states involved, primarily influenced by Interreg Programmes and the Madrid Convention. Former city networks also played a role in the initial EGTCs, leveraging experienced personnel and long-standing transnational collaborations.

4.4 The National Trends

The legal standing and administrative role of cities differs across national contexts. The relationship between the national government and local authorities is undergoing significant transformations from enhanced cooperation in some cases to competition or to competitive collaboration and even indifference in others (Marchetti, 2021, pp. 52–53).

An example of *enhanced cooperation* between the national and local levels is provided by the US and Taiwan's experiences. In late 2019, the City and State Diplomacy Act was introduced into the US Congress, a bill designed to harness and maximize the impact of international engagement by US states and cities. This legislation has received bipartisan support in both the House and Senate. The Act proposes the creation of an Office of Subnational Diplomacy within the US State Department to support the diplomatic efforts of subnational leaders and in its text recognizes the "increasingly significant" role that these actors are playing in US foreign policy. Biden's administration promised collaboration and an open approach to federal–local relations. In any case, the Act is significant in signaling a concerted effort to institutionalize subnational diplomacy and maximize its impact through the provision of national expertise and resources (Pejic and Acuto, 2022). Furthermore, to raise Taipei's international profile, the City Government has joined some important international city networks in recent years. To date, Taipei is an official member of the UCLG & United Cities and Local Governments Asia-Pacific (UCLG-ASPAC), Sister Cities International (SCI), CITYNET, the Global Social Economy Forum (GSEF), and Asian Network of Major Cities 21 (ANMC21). Moreover, Taipei City has been regularly invited to international conferences, such as the World Cities Summit (WCS) and Asia Pacific Cities Summit (APCS). Given Taiwan's limitations in engaging in multilateral systems, Taipei has used this international engagement to advance the interests of, not only the city, but also Taiwan more broadly. The government of Taipei works closely with the national government to ensure that the city's international affairs policies align with those of the federal government. This engagement occurs on an ad hoc basis in the absence of an established mechanism or process (Kosovac et al., 2020).

In Spain, Law 2/2014, of 25 March, on Action and the State Foreign Service, provides that the local authorities may carry out activities abroad within the framework of the powers attributed to them by the Constitution and the laws. These instruments are reported on by competent state bodies to determine whether they fall within the framework of the competencies of the entities that sign them and require a prior report from the Ministry of Foreign Affairs, which, being mandatory, is sent to the local government. In Finland, municipalities have a long tradition of international cooperation. The closest cooperation is between the neighboring Nordic countries – Sweden and

Norway – where there has for decades been a free movement without passports, especially between Haparanda-Tornio, the twinned towns on the border of Sweden and Finland. Over a series of policy issues, there has been some discussion on whether there needs to be a state agreement defining the extent of cooperation, but that approach has been found to be quite complicated and is deemed better to let municipal levels deepen their international cooperation on a mutual basis. In Croatia, in accordance with the Local and Regional Self-Government Act, the decision of the representative body on the establishment of international cooperation is subject to supervision of legality by the state administration body, being competent for local and regional self-government, i.e., the Ministry of Justice and Public Administration. If the competent Ministry assesses that the decision on establishing international cooperation is not in accordance with the law, it will propose, within 8 days from its receipt, to the Government of the Republic of Croatia to revoke the decision. The Government may, within 30 days of receipt of the proposal from the Ministry, issue a reasoned decision, revoking the decision of the local authority. In France, if an agreement is signed between a local authority and a foreign counterpart, the agreement must be sent to the representative of the state. The representative of the state can refer these agreements to the administrative court if he/she considers that they do not comply with the legal framework or are in conflict with France's international commitments. However, this is not an a priori approval procedure, but an a posteriori control. In Belgium, no prior approval by the competent authorities is needed for local authorities to engage in international partnerships, except for EGTCs. In Poland, the Ministry of Foreign Affairs gives its assent to the international engagements of local authorities as regulated by the Act of 15 September 2000 (*Journal of Laws* of 2000, No. 91, item 1009, of 2002, No. 113, item 984). In the event of a discrepancy between the objectives of the state's foreign policy and the local policy of international cooperation, the Minister of Foreign Affairs may withdraw the state's consent. In Serbia, international cooperation between local authorities is regulated by the Law on Local Self-Government within the framework of the foreign policy of the Republic. In cooperation with the Republic Secretariat for Legislation, the Ministry for Local Self-government affairs established a procedure for obtaining the consent of the Government of the Republic of Serbia. The municipality's decision on international engagement is submitted to the Ministry to obtain the opinion of the competent authorities and make a proposal to the Government of the Republic of Serbia to adopt an Act giving consent to the municipal decision on engagement with international cooperation. After the Government's decision on giving its consent to the local council decision on the establishment of international cooperation, it is implemented by the mayor or the president of the municipality, i.e., a person authorized by the mayor to sign an agreement on cooperation with the local self-government agency of another country, in accordance with the provisions of Article 44, paragraphs 1 and 5 of the Law, which provides that he is authorized to represent the local self-government agency and pass individual Acts. Last, but not least, in Greece, according to the provisions of articles 219–221 of the Code of Municipalities and Communities (L. 3463/2006) and the similar articles 96 and 101 of the "Kallikratis Programme" (L.3852/2010), which restructured territorial entities through the mergers of local authorities, municipalities cooperate with respective local government organizations, within the framework of their competences, for their participation in European and international networks of cities, town-twinnings, European and international programs, EGTCs, as well as in cultural and sports events and agreements to address issues of common interest. In accordance with the provisions of articles 219 par.3 and 220 par.3 of L. 3463/2006, the interministerial tripartite Committee of article 4 par. 2b of L. 3345/2005 is the competent body of the Hellenic Republic central government for the examination of the compatibility of the international initiatives of the municipalities with national policies, national and EU legislation, within the scope of their competences and the international obligations of the country. In fact, prior to any formalization of municipalities' international engagements, the consent of the above Committee is required. The Committee is composed of representatives from the Ministry of Interior (chair), the Ministry of Foreign Affairs, and the Central Union of Municipalities of Greece (Karvounis, 2023, pp. 146–156).

This cooperative relationship between central and local governments can take a highly political tone. Swedish cities reviewed and even halted their cooperation with Chinese towns amid deterioration in relations between the two countries in a fight over free expression, human rights and the fate of a Hong Kong publisher and Swedish citizen who had been sentenced after being held on charges of "endangering national security" (Milne, 2020). Furthermore, the city of Osaka ended its 60-year "sister city" relationship with San Francisco after the US city agreed to recognize the "comfort women" statue, which was erected by a private group in San Francisco's Chinatown district, as public property (McCurry, 2018). Additionally, on 15 March 2017, the Istanbul Metropolitan Municipality city council unanimously terminated its sister city protocol with the Netherlands's port city of Rotterdam amid an ongoing diplomatic row between the two countries. Istanbul and Rotterdam signed the town-twinning protocol on 24 June 2005. The diplomatic row between the two countries was stoked on 11 March 2017, when the Netherlands canceled the flight permit for Foreign Minister Mevlüt Çavuşoğlu for a meeting in the country. Later in the day, Family Minister Fatma Betül Sayan Kaya was prevented by Dutch police from reaching Turkey's consulate in Rotterdam after being told not to enter the Netherlands to conduct political campaigning for the 16 April charter referendum on shifting Turkey to an executive presidential system. Also, the Prague city council voted in October 2019 to cancel a partnership agreement with Beijing because the Chinese Capital rejected a Czech request to remove a clause from the agreement that states that Prague supports the one-China principle, which does not recognize Taiwan.

On the other hand, this relationship can become rather competitive. For instance, mayors of cities including Los Angeles, Atlanta, and Salt Lake City submitted a plan to the United Nations pledging to meet the US greenhouse gas emissions targets under the Paris climate accord, despite President Trump's decision in 2017 to withdraw from the agreement. In addition, the over 90 Sister City arrangements that Australian local governments have with Chinese cities came under scrutiny during a Senate inquiry into the legislation, especially in light of recent political tension between the nations. In late 2020, the government introduced and quickly passed Australia's Foreign Relations (State and Territory Arrangements) Bill 2020. This legislation sets up a regime which provides that public entities in Australia, including state and local governments and public universities, must report all arrangements they make with foreign entities, including foreign national, state, and local governments and state universities. The Australian federal government has the opportunity to review these arrangements and unilaterally cancel them if they are deemed to be incongruent with "Australia's foreign policy". This legislation is widely understood to be in response to the decision of the Victorian Government, one of Australia's state governments, to sign a memorandum of understanding with the Chinese government regarding the Belt and Road Initiative (Pejic and Acuto, 2022). Last, but not least, Zurich, as a member of the network of European cities that favored drug policies, opposed to the prohibitionist policies advanced by the Swiss federal government (Marchetti, 2021, p. 56).

4.5   Conclusions

Cities are entirely absent from the increasingly anachronistic international political and legal framework forged after World War II. Consequently, they have been forced to work within a system that largely denies their independent existence, or, more precisely, views them as subordinate appendages of their nation-states. States, not cities, are expected to represent their citizens and all subnational entities at the international level: national governments, not local ones, send representatives to staff the governing bodies comprising the United Nations and other international organizations, and states, not cities, are tasked with drafting, codifying, and enforcing international treaties and agreements on behalf of their subnational entities. Formally and institutionally, cities have no voice. On the other hand, cities, through their use of soft law instruments, savvy strategies, and influential alliances, are acquiring more and more soft power in the global sphere, allowing them to contribute, not only to the implementation and enforcement of global agendas and international law, but also to contribute to their very formation (Swiney, 2020).

References

Amilhat-Szary, A.-L., and Fourny, M.-C. (2006) *Après les frontières, avec la frontière. Nouvelles dynamiques transfrontalières en Europe*, La Tour d'Aigues: L'Aube.

Bages Bechade, S. (2003) "L'Europe soutien du développement des relations transfrontalières". In F. Bartczak and J. Rage (Eds.) *Les Pyrénées entre deux mondes* (pp. 45–55). Perpignan: Presses universitaires de Perpignan.

Bataillou, C. (2002) *L'émergence du fait régional au sein de l'Union européenne: la coopération trans-frontière comme stratégie de développement*. Perpignan: Presses.

Committee of the Regions (2001) *Trans-European Cooperation between Territorial Authorities. New Challenges and Future Steps Necessary to Improve Cooperation*, Brussels: CoR.

Committee of the Regions (2007) *The European Grouping of Territorial Cooperation-EGTC, CdR 117/2007*, Brussels: CoR

Committee of the Regions (2018a) *EGTC Monitoring Report 2017*, Brussels: CoR.

Committee of the Regions (2018b) *EGTC Good Practice Booklet*, Brussels: CoR.

Council of Europe (1980) *Explanatory Report to the European Outline Convention on Transfrontier Co-operation between Territorial Communities or Authorities*, Madrid, 21 May.

Council of Europe (1985a) *European Charter of Local Self-Government*, Strasbourg: CoE.

Council of Europe (1985b) Explanatory report of the European Charter of Local Self-Government (CETS No 122). http://conventions.coe.int/Treaty/en/Reports/Html/122.htm. Accessed 20 October 2022.

Council of Europe (1995) *Additional Protocol to the European Outline Convention on Transfrontier Co-operation between Territorial Communities or Authorities*, Strasbourg, 9 November.

Council of Europe (1998) *Protocol No. 2 to the European Outline Convention on Transfrontier Cooperation between Territorial Communities or Authorities concerning interterritorial cooperation*, Strasbourg, 5 May.

Council of Europe (2009) *Protocol No. 3 to the European Outline Convention on Transfrontier Cooperation between Territorial Communities or Authorities concerning Euroregional Cooperation Groupings (ECGs)*, Utrecht, 16 November.

De Sousa, L. (2012) "Understanding European Cross-Border Cooperation: A Framework for Analysis", *Journal of European Integration*, 35 (6), pp. 669–687.

GareSché, E.D.Z. (2007) *Guidelines for the international relations of local governments and decentralised cooperation between the European Union and Latin America*, Vol.1, Practical Manual for the Internationalisation of Cities, Diputación de Barcelona.

Jacob, L. (2013) "Territorial Thinking and the Legal Framework in Cross-Border Cooperation: The Recent Situation and Fieldwork Results in the Western Alps", *European Journal of Geography*, 4 (4), pp. 20–32.

Karvounis, A. (2023) *City Diplomacy and the Europeanisation of Local Government. The Prospects of Networking in the Greek Municipalities*, Cham: Palgrave.

Kosovac, A., Hartley, K., Acuto, M., and Gunning, D. (2020) *Conducting City Diplomacy. A Survey of International Engagement in 47 Cities*, Chicago-Parkville: The Chicago Council on Global Affairs & Connected Cities Lab.

La Porte, T. (2013) "City Public Diplomacy in the European Union". In M.K.D. Cross and J. Melissen (Eds.) *European Public Diplomacy. Soft Power at Work* (pp. 85–111). New York: Palgrave Macmillan.

Malcolm, E., and Bort, E. (1998) *The Frontiers of the European Union*, London: Pinter.

Marchetti, R. (2021) *City Diplomacy. From City-States to Global Cities*, Ann Arbor: University Michigan Press.

McCurry, J. (2018) "Osaka drops San Francisco as sister city over 'comfort women' statue", *The Guardian*, 4 October (https://www.theguardian.com/world/2018/oct/04/osaka-drops-san-francisco-as-sister-city-over-comfort-women-statue). Accessed 20 October 2022.

Milne, R. (2020) "Swedish cities cut China links after increase in tension", *Financial Times*, 25 February (https://www.ft.com/content/b6c8d510-429e-11ea-a43a-c4b328d9061c). Accessed 20 October 2022.

Papisca, A. (2008) "International Lawand Human Rights as a Legal Basis for the International Involvement of Local Governments". In A. Musch et al. (Eds.) *City Diplomacy: The Role of Local Governments in Conflict Prevention, Peace-Building PostConflict Reconstruction*, The Hague: VNG International

Pejic, D., and Acuto, M. (2022) "City Diplomacy Back Home: Central-Local Tensions in a Time of Global Urban Governance", *Journal of International Affairs*, 74 (1), pp. 23–39.

Scott, J.W. (2006) *EU Enlargement, Region Building and Shifting Borders of Inclusion and Exclusion*, Burlington: Ashgate.

Scott, J.W. (2012) "European Politics of Borders, Border Symbolism and Cross-Border Cooperation". In T.M. Wilson and H. Donnan (Eds.) *A Companion to Border Studies* (pp. 81–99). New York: Wiley-Blackwell.

Soós, E. (2013) "Contribution of EGTCs to Multilevel Governance", *International Journal of Multidisciplinary Thought*, 3 (3), pp. 519–531.

Swiney, C. (2020) "The Urbanization of International Law and International Relations: The Rising Soft Power of Cities in Global Governance", *Michigan Journal of International Law*, 41 (2), pp. 227–278.

Part II

Traditional and Modern Trends of City Diplomacy

5 Town-Twinnings

5.1 Introduction

"A twinning is the coming together of two communities seeking, in this way, to take action with a European perspective in the aim of facing their problems and developing between themselves closer and closer ties of friendship". In these words, in 1951, Jean Bareth, a founding member of the Council of European Municipalities and Regions (CEMR), emphasized the values of twinning as friendship, cooperation, and mutual awareness among European peoples (CEMR, 2003). Originating post-World War II and during the Cold War, town-twinning initially aimed to foster cultural exchange, diaspora connections, and commercial development, evolving into a systematic city diplomacy effort with over 20,000 partnerships at the European level. Today, European town-twinning is seen as "forerunners of integration", being "ahead of states", a solution for sustainability challenges and a platform for local best practice exchanges. In January 2023, Italian President Sergio Mattarella and German President Frank-Walter Steinmeier announced the second edition of the award for city cooperation, launched a year earlier, recognizing civic engagement, culture, inclusion, and sustainability.[1] The city of Zaragoza in Spain established a partnership with Ounck, a small Senegalese town. Geopolitical tensions prompted town-twinning, with Kyiv twinning with over 60 cities globally amid Russia's war on Ukraine. This allowed exchanges in education, ecology, tourism, economy, and communal services reform. Kyiv also received support from Riga (humanitarian aid and buses), Bergamo (restoration of communal infrastructure), Warsaw (cars), Prague (wagon of foods, heat guns, generators), and Budapest (children care).[2] Thus, rather than searching for alternative and more peaceful forms, town-twinning is part of a broader trend of togetherness and unity, with cities often leading national policies. In contrast, the US faces challenges in the economic dimension of twinning due to security considerations. China's Belt and Road Initiative complements sister-city partnerships, promoting Chinese outward FDI (foreign direct investment). In Africa, colonial legacies shape cross-border city connections (Han et al., 2021). While change and diversity provide the main

DOI: 10.4324/9781003470908-8

thread of town-twinnings, it is reasonable here to outline, first, a historical account and a conceptual framework that accommodates the various approaches explored and discussed in the different contributions and second explore the success factors and the practicalities to set up a town-twinning partnership.

5.2   The Historical Course of Town-Twinnings

Town-twinning, the oldest and most recognized form of international cooperation among local authorities, dates back to the first half of the 19th century (Karvounis, 2023, p. 60). In 1836, the informal twinning between the German city of Paderborn and the French city of Le Mans marked its inception. The first official modern twinning occurred in 1930, a century later, between the German city of Wiesbaden and the Austrian city of Klagenfurt (CEC, 1997). The early 20th century saw the formalization of bilateral relationships in city diplomacy, leading to "sister city" relationships or "town-twinning". Historically, Orléans (France) and Dundee (the United Kingdom) in 1946 are often cited as the first modern twinning arrangement, driven by the desire to strengthen the European idea and revive a 700-year-old alliance known as the "Auld" Alliance (CEC, 2003). Town-twinning emerged as a pacifist movement in the aftermath of World War II, symbolizing reconciliation and solidarity. The Council of Bristol's goodwill mission to Hanover in 1947 and subsequent agreements between Bordeaux and Bristol, as well as Velettes-sur-mer and Greenock, exemplified this sentiment. Town-twinning progressed alongside the promotion of the European idea, supported by the CEMR and the United Town Organization (UTO). In 1951, the CEMR was established as the largest European forum for local and regional authorities, while the Treaty of Rome in 1957 emphasized the commitment to a closer union among European peoples. The introduction of direct elections for European Parliament members in 1979 increased the influence of this representative body. In the same year, the Congress of Local and Regional Authorities of the Council of Europe recommended intensified efforts in town-twinning, advocating its use for inter-municipal assistance and encouraging citizen participation. In 1984, the European Council established a committee to address citizens' expectations and promote European identity. The Adonnino report highlighted the role of town-twinning in fostering solidarity and cooperation among European citizens. In 1988, the European Parliament acknowledged town-twinning's role in European unification and cultural network building, despite challenges, such as language barriers and geographical distances (CEC, 1997). The European Commission initiated the grants for town-twinnings in 1989, supporting projects under various European programs (see Europe for Citizens 2007–2013, 2014–2020, CERV, 2021–2027). Changes in central Europe after 1989 led to a proliferation of twinning links, contributing to the EU's enlargement in 2004 and fostering unity among the long-divided peoples of the Continent.

On the other side of the Atlantic, the "Sister Cities" program originated in 1956 under President Dwight Eisenhower. Initially part of the National League of Cities, it became an independent entity in 1967 known as Sister Cities International (SCI). SCI, a nonprofit citizen diplomacy network, focuses on establishing and strengthening partnerships between the US and international communities. The organization aims to enhance global cooperation at the municipal level, foster cultural understanding, and stimulate private business and economic development. Before the formalization of SCI, sister city relationships had already been established, such as the one between Toledo (Spain) and Toledo, Ohio (US) in 1931, and between Vancouver (Canada) and the Ukrainian city of Odessa in 1944. The latter relationship was forged to support the allied port city during the Second World War.

Alongside reconciliation goals, bilateral city diplomacy quickly deployed to create new partnerships between cities in the North and the South of the world, complementing a core goal of long-term solidarity with cultural and friendship purposes. The first town-twinning agreement between a French and an African city was signed in 1958 by Marseille and Abidjan. In France this process also involved small and medium cities: Millau (Aveyron) signed a twinning agreement with Louga (regional capital in North-western Senegal) in 1963 and in 1967 Loudun (Vienne) twinned with Ouagadougou, capital of Burkina Faso (Grandi, 2020, p. 40).

5.3 The Research on Town-Twinning

Over the years town-twinning has attracted a considerable amount of attention among researchers representing various academic disciplines (De Villiers, 2005). First, there have been numerous case studies, both investigating the phenomenon from the perspective of border studies (Ehlers, 2007), or from specific traditional academic disciplines (political science, sociology, economy, international relations, and so on) (Joenniemi, 2014). Second, a limited number of publications try to generalize town-twinning (Langenohl, 2015), mainly in Northern Europe (Anischenko and Sergunin, 2012; Joenniemi and Sergunin, 2011; Lundén, 2004) and in Central Europe (Jańczak, 2013b). Some, especially recently, try to compare more cases in the Old Continent (Jańczak, 2013a; Schultz et al., 2002), in North America (Guhathakurta et al., 2010), in Africa and in Asia (Mikhailova, 2013). Single texts compare town-twinning in various continents (Nugent, 2012; Zelinsky, 1991). Third, with a purpose to promote cultural exchange, the sister-city movement is seen as a powerful element of the "'quiet revolution' in local governance" (World Bank, 2000, pp. 154–155) and allows "synergy and the combining of resources among the public sector, international organizations, the voluntary and community sector, individuals and households" (World Bank, 2000, p. 155). As a bilateral partnership, town-twinning relationship, linking two local communities from different countries, can serve the function to reduce the cultural barrier, bridging the global local divide (Cremer et al., 2001). This partnership that deserves greater recognition from both domestic and global perspectives has been largely ignored by the existing body of research (O'Toole, 2001). Baycan-Levent et al. (2008) conduct a survey based on European cities and their sister-cities and find that the number of visitors, students, cultural activities, and economic cooperation with entrepreneurs has increased in 50% of these cities after the agreement is signed. In particular, they find that the remarkable increase in the number of visitors by 59% and students by 52% is due to the cultural exchange introduced by sister cities. In a similar vein, Ramasamy and Cremer (1998) investigate the town-twinning relationship between New Zealand and a number of Asian countries likewise. According to their survey, the town-twinning partnership reduces the cultural differences. These studies all provide evidence on the cultural communication driven by the town-twinning partnership.

This concise account of the research on town-twinnings appears to be quite challenging, with town-twinning being in general difficult to capture, due to its rather fluid forms. It not only transcends state-centered forms of spatialization and the understanding of state boundaries as the demarcations of social, community, and political life. It also cannot be captured by many of the standard categories ordinarily applied in analyzing the unfolding of political space. Not only do an ever increasing number of cities pursue policies that combine the local and international under the heading of town-twinning, they have also emancipated themselves by generating a broad variety of ways of town-twinning, as the various endeavors to conceptualize it betray.

5.4   The Concept of Town-Twinnings

Overall, the concept of "twin cities" appears to lack a broadly agreed meaning, and it also appears that this nebulous meaning has shifted over time (FMCU-UTO, 2003). For example, Köhle (2005, p. 16) identifies a gradual change on the European scene from "partnerships of reconciliation" to "partnerships of integration". Instead of a merely symbolic emphasis on togetherness, the aim appears to be increasingly shifting toward concrete and functional cooperation. O'Toole (2001, p. 405) delineates distinct stages in the evolution of town-twinnings. Early definitions emphasize friendship, while later ones incorporate economic development aspects. The three interconnected phases are as follows: *Associative phase*: primarily based on friendship and cultural exchange; *reciprocative phase*: Involves educational and people exchanges, developing skills among participants; *commercial exchange phase*: focuses on economic development without abandoning the earlier phases; aims to leverage the process for local economic goals. The South African Municipal International Relations Policy Framework (DPLG, 1999, p. 7) notes a shift in municipal cooperation toward more substantial, project-focused activities with measurable objectives.

The plurality of interpretations has approached town-twinning figures as a rather vexed question in the research literature. Different schools, countries suggest different interpretations and employ various synonyms: sister cities (US, Mexico), twin cities (Russia, United Kingdom), friendship cities (as with relations between Japanese and Chinese cities), partnerstadt (Germany), and jumelage (France) (SCI, 2002). More than one city could be twinned with a city (multiple twinning). Three cities in one agreement are also common (called trinning). The propensity for multiple twinning is roughly associated with population size, according to Zelinsky (1991, p. 4).

Thus, one definition has taken city twinning to mean the domestic phenomenon of proximate urban centers agglomerating over time, while internationally focused definitions are split between broad and narrow perspectives of twinning, with the term "twin city" itself being merely the most common term among many others (Buursink, 2001; Schultz et al., 2002). The broad definition describes cooperative arrangements between cities, towns, and even non-adjacent countries, promoting economic and cultural ties. Such forms of twinning occur primarily between cities sharing similar social, economic and political patterns and structures, and/or historical links.

Also, more refined distinctions have been introduced. Buursink (2001), for example, has introduced a division between "town couples" that aim at far-reaching cooperation and those with a more competitive relationship. Schultz et al. (2002), in turn, claim that only the so-called "double-towns" can be seen as real twins and set a number of criteria for defining such towns. Accordingly, "double towns" should consist of towns which also share a common history as homogenous administrative units prior to national borders separating them. In addition, she focuses on cases where urban entities face each other across a shared river, hence the synonymous term "bridge towns", and insists on the presence of other ethnic as well as cultural affinities. The World Health Organization (WHO, 2001, p. 2) quotes the TACIS definition of twinning which states: "Twinning is a formal and substantive collaboration between two organisations and/or cities".

In the concept of twinning, "town" and "city" refer not only to the local government or municipality, but the whole community, including civil society, the business community, and the education sector. The local government plays a very important facilitating role in setting up and maintaining the relationship, but the primary bond is forged between communities and not only between local governments. "Sister-city programs are unique in that they inherently involve the three main sectors in a community: local government, businesses, and a wide variety of citizen volunteers (and civil society or non-profit organisations)" (SCI, 2003, p. 2). According to Eric Gcabaza, another distinction between municipality-to-municipality relations and a sister-city agreement is that in a sister-city agreement, the mayor on behalf of the people or city, and not on behalf of the municipality, enters into the agreement (DPLG, 2003).

The United Nations Development Program defines town-twinning as "a long-term partnership between communities in different cities or towns", with an open agenda (UNDP, 2000, p. 8). According to the Local Government International Bureau of the United Kingdom (LGIB, 2001, p. 4), a town-twinning link is a "formal, long-term friendship agreement involving cooperation between two communities from different countries, and endorsed by both local authorities. The idea is that two communities organize projects and activities around a range of issues and develop an understanding of historical, cultural, lifestyle similarities and differences". They suggest, however, that the concept of transnational partnerships and town-twinning is difficult to define because it is not uniform or static. It is a multi-faceted, organic process which can be customized to meet the individual and specific needs of a community (LGIB, 2001, p. 4). According to the Institute of Economic Research in New Zealand (2003, p. 3), "sister city relationships are formal relationships between two cities from different countries". Sister city relationships use individual contact at the local level to promote communication across borders, and the aim is: "To stimulate cultural awareness and understanding in order to increase the flow of ideas and promoting cultural, educational and sporting exchange, as well as increasing tourism and trade between the two cities". The above conceptual endeavors lead us to realize when defining town-twinning that the concept has evolved radically over the last 50 years.

5.5 Practical Steps to Setting Up a Town-Twinning Partnership

In general, there are two main phases and practical steps in the process leading to town-twinning and each one requires equal attention and time (Handley, 2006):

5.5.1 *Motivation and Choice of a Partner*

Choosing a partner town for twinning should involve careful consideration of motivations. Initial factors often include similar or complementary structural features. It's essential to weigh the population size and geographical location of a potential partner town. Shared history, socio-cultural context, or linguistic similarities may also influence the choice. If no suitable match is found, national and European twinning organizations, such as CEMR, can be contacted for assistance. In Sino-British town-twinning initiatives, social motivations often involve the active engagement of business or civic organizations and educational institutions (Bartram and Xiang, 2013). Such initiatives typically stem from pre-existing collaborations between local organizations on both sides, with town-twinning seen as the next step to strengthen city-to-city relations. For example, the Sheffield-Chengdu town-twinning relationship, formalized in 2010, was facilitated by the connection between the football clubs Sheffield United FC and Chengdu Blades FC, along with support from Sheffield's local Chinese community, which played a crucial role after the

Szechuan earthquake in 2008. Educational bonds have also played a role in twinning arrangements, as seen in the case of Sunderland and Harbin, where formal town-twinning followed interactions between local schools. Additionally, economic compatibility guides the selection of twinning partners, as evident in the Taiyuan-Newcastle case, where shared coal resources led to collaboration in the sale of heavy equipment from the north-east coalfields to Taiyuan. Support from national and supranational government tiers has further encouraged Sino-British twinning relations. Both the Chinese and British national governments have utilized town-twinning to strengthen overall bilateral relationships. Former Chinese Prime Minister Wen Jiabao facilitated the agreement between the Welsh government and Chongqing in 2000, while UK Chancellor George Osborne highlighted existing town-twinning relations, such as Sheffield and Chengdu, as evidence of the close Sino-British relationship in a speech encouraging business partnerships between China and Northern England (Wu et al., 2016).

5.5.2 Initial Contacts and Exploratory Visit

Establishing contact between potential town-twinning partners is crucial for assessing common interests. Exploratory visits serve as a valuable means to discuss individual goals for the partnership and ensure consensus on the way forward. The preparatory stage involves exchanges of letters and various contacts, with both sides conducting basic research on each other's culture and compiling key questions. Before an official visit, delegations typically create a list of queries and engage in initial research. During the visit, the delegations decide the form the town-twinning arrangement will take and finalize practical details. Often, an initial exchange coincides with a cultural or sporting event, serving as a "courtship" period. Practical matters, beyond financial considerations, demand total commitment and enthusiasm from organizers in both towns. The actual town-twinning ceremony usually occurs a few months after the initial contacts, emphasizing the need for careful thought and planning to ensure maximum involvement from residents. Educational events may also be organized to enhance the twinning experience (Hsu, 2003).

5.5.3 Supporting Structure: The Town-Twinning Committee

The organization and promotion of the town-twinning procedures presupposes a supporting structure. This can be an integral part of the local administration or an independent association, usually known as the "town-twinning committee". The town-twinning committee constitutes the main body of coordination of the town-twinning activities, in which official representatives of the town, as well as inhabitants, on a voluntary basis, are involved (alternatively, NGOs or other citizens' associations). Volunteerism is the driving force of the international partnerships struck among local authorities. Whatever form the committee takes, the important point is to involve as many local interests as possible. Cultural, athletic, artistic, voluntary associations are always active and willing to organize and implement town-twinning activities. Moreover, schools, either through the teaching staff or with the assistance of students (e-twinning), play a key role in the exchanges among local authorities. The main tasks of the town-twinning committee are as follows:

- Preparation and coordination of the program of town-twinning activities.
- Calculation of the economic cost of the specific activities (transportation and accommodation expenses).
- Search for the requisite grant.
- Representation of the local society.
- Securing the active involvement of the citizens.
- Continuation of activities irrespective of the changes taking place at the level of local authority.

5.5.4 Practicalities

There are certain practical questions to be answered when contemplating a town-twinning arrangement, mainly in the following areas:

- *Sources of funding*
  Town-twinning requires financial investment, often sourced from local public finance or direct contributions. Participants can raise funds through events, donations, or professional advertising. The community's creativity and generosity significantly impact the town-twinning budget, and benefits in kind, such as loaned premises or voluntary services, play a role. External funding may come from grants, such as those from the European Commission's town-twinning promotion programs (e.g., CERV) or other specialized organizations for specific exchange projects.
- *Lodging with local people*
  Accommodation may at first seem a minor matter, but it has its part to play in making visitors from partner towns feel at home. Lodging with local families on a reciprocal basis is one of the principles of town-twinning. Staying in people's homes is not seen primarily as a means of keeping costs to a minimium; it is also, in fact mainly, a way of sharing the day-to-day lives of the people who live in the partner town. As well as being a chance to learn something of different customs, it creates the ideal setting for striking up new friendships. However, certain types of exchanges, or events which are well attended by people from the partner town, do sometimes mean that other forms of accommodation, such as hotels and youth hostels, have to be used.
- *Communication and information*
  Communication and information are pivotal in town-twinning, utilizing the internet, social media, and community involvement. An effective

supporting structure is essential for stimulating communication. Signposts at the town entrance displaying partner town names serve as a powerful tool for conveying the town-twinning message. Municipal news sheets, electronic display boards, local media, radio, television, and social platforms are employed to reach a wider audience. Stands representing partner towns strategically placed at local events enhance visibility. Town-twinning documentation, including translated brochures, fosters mutual understanding. Regular updates on the partner town also contribute to ongoing effective communication.

5.5.5   *Town-Twinning Ceremony and Oath*

The formalization of the relationship takes place at a ceremony where the mayor of each town signs a town-twinning oath, before the rest of the elected representatives as well as the members of the local societies. It is customary for the ceremony to be held first in the one town and then in the other, sometimes during the same year, but usually in two successive years. The town-twinning organizations, such as the CEMR and the UTO, can provide advice on organizing the event, particularly regarding the program content and the symbols to be used.

5.6   Conclusions

Although some sources suggest that town-twinnings have been superseded by more complex types of relationship forms in recent years, in many areas of the world the town-twinning model is not only in use but, according to the town-twinning organizations in both Europe, through the European Municipalities and Regions (CEMR), and the US, through SCI, is seen as a preferred model of interaction now and in the future. As a matter of fact, a recent report from CEMR (2023) demonstrates that town-twinning remains a relevant practice with an effective and meaningful impact. Almost 80% of the respondents expressed their intent to continue developing town-twinning activities, with the majority wishing to explore new partnership possibilities. This report also shows that the town-twinning experiences are not limited solely to the classic cultural context. While 50% of cities used town-twinning as a way to establish cultural connections with their peers, more than half reported using it as a springboard for developing sustainable networks, which are analyzed in the following chapter.

Notes

1 See https://urban-diplomacy.de/en/germany-italy/.
2 See https://visitukraine.today/blog/1399/sister-cities-of-kyiv-what-does-such-cooperation-and-the-essence-of-twinning-during-the-war-give.

References

Anischenko, A., and Sergunin, A. (2012) "Twin Cities: A New Form of Cross-Border Cooperation in the Baltic Sea Region?", *Baltic Region/Baltijskij Region*, 11, pp. 19–27.

Bartram and Xiang (2013) "A twin-win situation", *China Daily Europe*, 15 March, [Online], URL: https://www.chinadaily.com.cn/a/201303/15/WS5a2a1e6aa3101a51ddf8ebf8.html.

Baycan-Levent, T., Kundak, S., and Gulumser, A. (2008) "City-to-city Linkages in a Mobile Society: The Role of Urban Networks in Eurocities and Sister Cities", *International Journal of Services Technology and Management*, 10 (1), pp. 83–109.

Buursink, J. (2001) "The Binational Reality of Border-Crossing Cities", *Geojournal*, 54 (1), pp. 7–19.

CEC (1997) *A Europe of Towns and Cities. A Practical Guide to Town-Twinning*, Luxembourg: Office for Official Publications of the European Communities.

CEC (2003) "An Old Phenomenon Expanding Fast". In *The Magazine, Belonging to the European Union*, Issue 20. Luxembourg: Office for Official Publications of the European Communities.

CEMR (2003) *A Europe of Citizens. Tomorrow's Europe*, CCRE/CEMR, Paris: CEMR.

CEMR (2023) *Analysis of Twinning in Europe. Charting the Twinning of Tomorrow*, Paris: CEMR.

Cremer, R.D., De Bruin, A., and Dupuis, A. (2001) "International Sister Cities – Bridging the Global Local Divide", *American Journal of Economics and Sociology*, 60 (1), January, pp. 377–402.

De Villiers, J.C. (2005) *"Strategic alliances between communities, with special emphasis on the twinning of South African cities and towns with international partners"*, *Unpublished doctoral dissertation*, Graduate School of Business, University of Stellenbosch, Bellville Park Campus.

DPLG (Department of Provincial and Local Government) (1999) *Municipal International Relations – A Policy Framework for South Africa*, Pretoria: Ministry for Provincial and Local Government.

DPLG (Department of Provincial and Local Government) (2003) *Municipal twinning training workshop – notes*. Port Elizabeth, Eastern Cape Province, 31 July–1 August.

Ehlers, N. (2007) *The Binational City Eurode. The Social Legitimacy of a Border-Crossing Town*, Aachen: Shaker Verlag.

FMCU-UTO (World Federation of United and Twinned Towns) (2003) "What is city-city cooperation?" [Online] Available https://www.old.uclg.org/en/issues/city-city-cooperation.

Grandi, L.K. (2020) *City Diplomacy*, Cham: Palgrave Macmillan.

Guhathakurta, S., Pijawka, D., and Sadalla, E. (2010) *The Border Observatory Project. The State of U.S.-Mexico Border Cities*, Phoenix: Southwest Consortium for Environmental Research & Policy.

Handley, S. (2006) *Take Your Partners. The Local Authority Handbook on International Partnerships*, London: Local Government International Bureau.

Han, Y., Wang, H., and Wei, D. (2021) "The Belt and Road Initiative, Sister-City Partnership and Chinese Outward FDI", *Economic Research*, 35 (1), pp. 3416–3436.

Hsu, Y. (2003) *"Montreal's twinning with Shanghai – A case study of urban diplomacy in the global economy"*, *Unpublished doctoral dissertation in the department of communication studies*. Montreal, Quebec, Canada: Concordia University.

Jańczak, J. (2013a) *Border Twin Towns in Europe. Cross-Border Cooperation at a Local Level*, Berlin: Logos Verlag.

Jańczak, J. (2013b) "Revised Boundaries and Re-frontierization. Border Twin Towns in Central Europe", *Revue d'études comparatives Est-Ouest*, 44, pp. 53–92.

Joenniemi, P. (2014) "City-Twinning as Local Foreign Policy: The Case of Kirkenes – Nickel", *EUBorderScapes Working Paper*, 8, pp. 1–23.

Joenniemi, P., and Sergunin, A. (2011) "When Two Aspire to Become One: City-Twinning in Northern Europe", *Journal of Borderlands Studies*, 26 (2), pp. 231–242.

Karvounis, A. (2023) *City Diplomacy and the Europeanisation of Local Government. The Prospects of Networking in the Greek Municipalities*, Cham: Palgrave Macmillan.

Köhle, B. (2005) *Town Twinning. Jumelage. Kommunale Partnerschaften*, Wien: Universität zur Weiterbildung Krems.

Langenohl, A. (2015) *Town Twinning, Transnational Connection and Trans-Local Citizenship in Europe*, Houndmills: Palgrave Macmillan.

LGIB (Local Government International Bureau) (2001) "The links effect: a good practice guide to transnational partnerships and twinning of local authorities". *LGIB International report*, No 3, October.

Lundén, T. (2004) "European Twin Cities: Models, Examples and Problems of Formal and Informal Co-operation", *ISIG Quarterly of International Sociology*, pp. 1–14.

Mikhailova, E. (2013) "Appearance and Appliance of the Twin-cities Concept on the Russian-Chinese Border", *ISPRS - International Archives of the Photogrammetry, Remote Sensing and Spatial Information Sciences*, XL-4/W3, pp. 105–110.

New Zealand Institute of Economic Research (2003) *The economic benefits of sister city relationships: Report to Sister Cities New Zealand*, Wellington: New Zealand Institute of Economic Research [Online], URL: https://www.nzier.org.nz/publications/economic-benefits-of-sister-city-relationships#.

Nugent, P. (2012) "Border Towns and Cities in Comparative Perspective". In T. Wilson and H. Donnan (Eds.) *A Companion to Border Studies* (pp. 557–572). Oxford: Blackwell Publishing.

O'Toole, K. (2001) "Kokusaika and Internationalisation: Australian and Japanese Sister City Type Relationships", *Australian Journal of International Affairs*, 55 (3), pp. 403–419.

Ramasamy, B., and Cremer, R.D. (1998) "Cities, Commerce and Culture – The Economic Role of International Sister-City Relationships between New Zealand and Asia", *Journal of the Asia Pacific Economy*, 3 (3), pp. 446–461.

Schultz, H., Stokłosa, K., and Jajeśniak-Quast, D. (2002) "Twin Towns on the Border as Laboratories of European Integration", *FIT Discussion Paper*, 4, pp. 1–74.

SCI (Sister Cities International) (2002) "Sister Cities – At the cutting edge of economic and community development". Washington. [Online]. URL: https://sistercities.org.

SCI (Sister Cities International) (2003) "What are sister cities?" [Online]. URL: https://sistercities.org.

UNDP (United Nations Development Programme) (2000) "The challenges of linking". Bureau for Development Policy. [Online]. URL: https://www.undp.org/development-challenges-and-solutions.

WHO (World Health Organization) Regional Office for Europe (2001) *Guidelines for city twinning*, Copenhagen, Denmark.

World Bank (2000) *World Development Report. 1999/2000: Entering the 21st Century*, Oxford: Oxford University Press.

Wu, F., Zhang, F., and Wang, Z. (2016) *Twinning and Contact between British and Chinese Cities*, London: Government Office for Science.

Zelinsky, W. (1991) "The Twinning of the World: Sister Cities in Geographic and Historical Perspective", *Annals of the Association of American Geographers*, 81 (1), pp. 1–31.

6 City Networks

6.1 Introduction

Cities have become crucial players in global affairs, engaging in peacemaking and utilizing soft power strategies alongside nation-states. In addition to traditional global cities associated with nation-states and corporations, cities coordinate their concerns and interests through city networks. The surge in city-to-city diplomatic initiatives over the past three decades has seen a significant rise in organized associations of cities globally. Cities are increasingly recognized for addressing global challenges, from climate change to cybersecurity and pandemics (Bansard et al., 2016). Cities, rather than nations, have become pioneers in diplomatic relations, marking a significant evolution in global governance and cooperation (Karvounis, 2011). The former mayor of Melbourne, Robert Doyle, aptly captures this shift, stating that "nations speak, cities act" (Curtis, 2016, p. 4). Chinese cities, such as Guangzhou, actively participate in global city agendas and transnational networks, contributing to China's efforts to open up and experiment (Klaus and Curtis, 2020). A recent research developed by the Melbourne Centre for Cities at the University of Melbourne on the types of international engagement that have had the greatest impact on their city's policymaking found that city networking was overwhelmingly the most popular, selected by 81% of cities, whereas twinning/sister city programs were second (41%) (Pejic et al., 2022). "[B]y coming together in transnational networks, cities have offered the possibility of an emergent political assemblage that can offer forms of governance that can match the scale and complexity of global challenges" (Curtis & Acuto, 2018, p. 12). For example, city networks are replacing nation states as the driving force behind climate change policy development and implementation strategies (Curtis & Acuto, 2018). City networks, such as C40, signal a notable departure from traditional city-to-city cooperation, embracing more entrepreneurial, public-private "hybrid" urban policies reminiscent of pre-modern city-states (Pipa and Bouchet, 2021). These contemporary networks extend beyond town-twinning initiatives such as Sister Cities International (SCI), forming partnerships with international organizations and integrating with

DOI: 10.4324/9781003470908-9

private sector initiatives. In this sense, the theme of the 1980 Toronto conference, "Thinking Globally, Acting Locally", remains relevant today. This chapter examines city networking as a major form of city diplomacy through its historical, theoretical, and practical aspects.

6.2 The Historical Evolution of the International City Networks

The International Union of Local Authorities (IULA), now known as the United Cities and Local Governments (UCLG), originated during the 1913 World Exhibition in Ghent, Belgium. As the first international cities organization, IULA aimed to foster common ideas among cities (Tavares, 2016, p. 11). Following World War II, the first IULA postwar Congress took place in Paris in 1947, where the Union International des Maires was founded by French and German mayors to promote goodwill and peace (Balbim, 2016, p. 140). IULA remained active until 2003 when it merged with the United Towns Organization (UTO) to form UCLG on 1 January 2004. UCLG plays a crucial role in advocacy, representing local governments and advancing their interests globally.

The postwar era also witnessed the formation of the Council of European Municipalities (CEMR) in 1951 and SCI in 1956. These organizations contributed to the rise of city networks, serving as forums for collective action and advocacy. Inspired by historical models, such as the Hanseatic League, city networks aimed to ensure that urban and local voices were heard on the global stage, leading to the emergence of various international associations of cities (Acuto et al., 2021, p. 140).

In Europe, the European Commission advocated for the creation of European local and regional networks as early as 1989. By the 1990s, the EU had developed a multilevel governance framework through networks to implement place-sensitive programs (Giest and Howlett, 2013, p. 342). The Maastricht Treaty, the principle of subsidiarity, the establishment of the Committee of the Regions (CoR), and cross-border cooperation programs (INTERREG) played pivotal roles in this development.

The late years of the Cold War and the early 1990s witnessed a mix of "first generation" city diplomacy forms, such as Mayors for Peace (1982), and novel forms, such as the International Council for Local Environmental Initiatives (ICLEI) founded in 1990. These initiatives marked a shift from symbolic town-twinning to more practical diplomatic activities involving thousands of local governments worldwide (Acuto et al., 2021, p. 140; Kosovac et al., 2020, p. 6).

Cities started to assume more significant global responsibilities around the turn of the century, connected to major global priorities. An ecosystem of enduring public membership networks such as Eurocities and Energy Cities evolved into a complex system, including multiactor networks operating on a global scale (Fernández de Losada, 2019, p. 19). Private-led city platforms, exemplified by the Global Parliament of Mayors and multiactor platforms, such as Cities Alliance, emerged, emphasizing varied leadership and diversified composition (Acuto, 2020).

At the forefront of this evolution are privately led city platforms, such as C40, supported by Bloomberg Philanthropies, and 100 Resilient Cities (100RC), established by the Rockefeller Foundation. These platforms offer cities skilled multidisciplinary teams without charging fees, but lack the reach and representativeness of traditional city networks, posing challenges and raising questions about the current ecosystem of city networks (Acuto et al., 2021, p. 143). Despite these challenges, scholarly attention on city networking remains fragmented and incomplete.

6.3   The Conceptualization of the International City Networks

Several definitions of city networks have been proposed in recent years. City networks have been widely understood in the literature as formal or less formal collaborative initiatives to share information and disseminate experiences in urban policy, management, and sustainable development (Labaeye and Sauer, 2013, p. vii). In other words, these are mainly bottom-up initiatives whose global role is widely acknowledged. There is a well-developed body of work on city networking, especially, in the context of environmental and sustainability initiatives (Bouteligier, 2013) and an often less advertised, but refined scholarship, linked directly to WHO Healthy Cities looking at health policy in cities in a networked way (De Leeuw, 2001). There is even some scholarly and practical writing on the role of city networking in traditional international relations (IR) arenas, such as conflict and security (Mush, 2008). However, these remain "silo-ed" approaches, failing to take into account the complexity and breadth of city networks across different sectors (Acuto et al., 2017, p. 15). Several other contributions to the literature appear highly descriptive in their attempt to identify and categorize the actions of the networks (Ercole et al., 1997). In this respect, the literature is particularly focused on funding as the most visible incentive for city networking membership (Benington and Harvey, 1994, pp. 946–947; Lawrence, 2000); the exchange of good practices and the drawing up of innovative policies (Labaeye and Sauer, 2013, p. 6; Payre, 2010; Roca, 2019, p. 69; Salskov-Iversen, 2006a, 2006b); the formation of European identity (Phelps et al., 2002), while also being connected to new public management practices; and the legitimacy of local public policies (Camps, 2019).

Apart from their functions, city networks can be approached by their internal organization, focusing on their structures (horizontal, vertical, and polycentric) (Dematteis, 1994; Dematteis and Guarrasi, 1995). Kern and Bulkeley (2009) propose three criteria for city networks: voluntary membership, a polycentric setup for self-governance, and functions beyond lobbying to help members implement policies. Busch (2015) adds criteria of having more than two members and a certain degree of formalization and institutionalization. Barber (1997, p. 22) underlined that these networks, such as Cities Alliance, are not limited to recruiting only local government bodies, but include a range of actors, such as universities, chambers of commerce, and private sector bodies (Abdullah and Garcia-Chueca, 2020; Acuto et al., 2017, p. 38); they also require the active role and support of elected officials and often have an office in strategic locations, acting as an "embassy" and representation of local councils (John, 1994).

On the other hand, as Lawrence (2000, p. 65) noted, most networks face language and leadership deficits and costs, engaging in these functions and practices. Bouteligier's research also concluded that deficits in the implementation of good practices have less to do with cities' similarities or differences than with power relations within networks where a small group of cities dictates the agenda to the rest of their partners (Bouteligier, 2013, p. 59). In fact, it is argued that city networks are often animated by a few key cities that are sustainability leaders or pioneers (Bouteligier, 2013; Keiner and Kim, 2007). More precisely, among city networks, Keiner and Kim (2007) distinguish the "giving end" – the frontrunner cities that figure prominently coordinating and undertaking responsibility – and the "receiving end", which get involved only to access networking resources. Following this thread, various publications point out that transnational municipal networks are often "networks of pioneers for pioneers" (Kern and Bulkeley, 2009). Likewise, Aall et al. (2007, p. 99) warn policymakers of situations where an "island of 'best practice' is surrounded by a sea of 'business-as-usual', and thus serve as a 'lightening rod' to distract attention from a passive national policy". Also, Curtis (2014, p. 29) argues that none of the multilateral initiatives of cities at the international level have produced particularly impressive global governance outcomes. Malé (2019, p. 36) suggests that thematic city network platforms develop as effective interchange mechanisms among local authorities, but not as tools for structural transformation and change.

Bearing in mind the above, we could, in general, argue that city networks have gone beyond mere bilateral agreements or town-twinnings in terms of scope, goals, and composition. They include municipal and non-municipal actors (regions, think tanks, NGOs, private sector, etc.) and provide the necessary infrastructure for cities to operate at the international level, addressing a large list of policy issues, either on a temporary or permanent basis. In this respect, and on the elements collected by the aforementioned definitions, we can suggest that *an international network of cities is a voluntary, multilateral, multi-stakeholder, transnational cooperation between local authorities and other non-municipal actors, more or less organizationally structured, oriented toward one (single-issue or mono-actoral city networks) or more issues (multi-purpose networks) of common interest, and aims to improve the operational dynamics of all participating parties through exchange of actions, influence and targeted projects, in the short or long term* (Karvounis, 2023, p. 63).

6.4   The Typology of the International City Networks

The conceptualization of city networks has led to the development of various typologies in the literature, serving as frameworks for analysis and evaluation. Typologies facilitate quantitative and comparative research by providing clear concepts for measurement and addressing diverse phenomena. They also aid in clarifying and defining new concepts from a qualitative perspective (Lara, 2020, p. 196). However, simplifying the diverse nature of city networks into predefined typologies can result in distortions, given their hybrid and dynamic nature.

One typology, proposed by Bouteligier (2013, pp. 19–21), distinguishes between two major types of city networks for global governance. The first type emerges from the location and organization strategies of global actors, where cities play strategic roles. The second type is established to address common urban challenges efficiently, with local authorities cooperating by exchanging knowledge and experiences (e.g., Cities Alliance, Cities without Slums, Global Cities Dialogue). Both of these categories contain networks of varying weight and scope. Some cover a wide range of topics ("multi-thematic"), such as Eurocities, while others focus on a single issue (e.g., LUCI-Lighting Urban Community International). Kristin Kern (2007, p. 18) adds another type related to EU programs, while Michele Acuto and Steve Rayner (2016, p. 1150) emphasize that city networks can be considered only those formal organizations that include cities as their core members and are characterized by mutual and recognized communication patterns and processes of policy planning and exchanges (e.g., C40). Such a perception of international city networks, however, negates a key feature of these forms of networked governance, that is, the partnership of public and private actors that highlights the new hybrid type of city networks.

Fernández de Losada (2019) provides a concise typology of the current ecosystem of city networks, including generalist global public membership networks (e.g., UCLG, Metropolis), regional generalist public membership networks (e.g., Eurocities, Union of Baltic Cities), networks linked to cultural communities (e.g., AIMF, CLFG), specialized global public membership networks (e.g., ICLEI, Cities Alliance), thematic regional public membership networks (e.g., Polis), mixed or multi-level publicly led networks (e.g., CityNet), and privately led networks (e.g., C40, 100RC, Global Parliament of Mayors).

Other contributions to the literature have distinguished city networks based on hierarchy (Boix, 2003, p. 4), collaboration and complementarity (Camagni and Salone, 1993), expertise (Trullén and Boix, 2003), geographic scope, policy scope, and duration. Different classifications have been proposed by Rizzo (2002) and Leffe and Acuto (2017). The former ranks city networks according to the following criteria: (a) geographic scope; (b) policy scope; (c) number of participating members; (d) benefits and services to members; (e) current initiatives and achievements; (f) presence of an intergovernmental network structure; (g) adequacy of available resources as well as linkages with local/international institutions and organizations; and (h) their contribution to quality of life within the geographical area covered. The latter classify city networks according to the public policy field: city networks focused on broad governance issues (e.g., UCLG, Metropolis); city networks focused on more general aspects of environmental protection (e.g., ICLEI); city networks focused on specific environmental issues (e.g., Partnerships in Environmental Management for the Seas of East Asia Network of Local Governments); city networks focused on climate change (e.g., C40); and city networks focused on regional and policy issues (e.g., EFUS, European Healthy Cities). Last but not least, Karvounis (2023, p. 65) categorized EU city networks, according to the organization that took the initiative to form them, as such: Traditional city networks (e.g., Eurocities, Energy Cities, Union of Baltic Cities, Eurotowns); EU-led city networks (e.g., Reference Framework for European Sustainable Cities), which cannot be confused with the so-called "EU-led Campaigns", such as Covenant of Mayors, Covenant of Island Areas, Smart Cities and Communities – European Innovation Partnership, etc.; internationally led city networks (e.g., European network of Health Cities of WHO, Coalition of Cities against Racism of UNESCO); and project-bound city networks (e.g., URBACT city networks). In the same vein, Balbim (2021) argued that the city networks could be classified as project networks, corporate networks (e.g., Leading Cities, Global Cities Initiative, Urban Land Institute, NY Global Partners, 100 Resilient Cities, The Indus Entrepreneurs), and self-governed city networks (e.g., UCLG; Metropolis; C40; World Network of Port Cities; and International Association of Educating Cities).

While these typologies provide valuable frameworks for analysis, it's crucial to recognize the fluid and dynamic nature of city networks, which constantly adapt to evolving policy and governance scenarios.

6.5 Practical Steps to Setting Up an International City Network

As in the case of town-twinnings, the setting up of a city network goes through various phases.

- *Definition of the pursued aim (rationale)*
  Before resorting to anything else, the vision and the reason that render necessary the setting up of an international network must be clearly articulated.

- *Ensuring support*
  Securing strong and broad support from local, regional, national and international political, social, and economic agencies constitutes a form of a sustainability guarantee.
- *Finding partners*
  The search for partners depends on the character of the network (single thematic or multithematic, regional, corporate), and previous relationships (see town-twinnings, partners in a project).
- *Formalization of the relationship (agreement)*
  Following the agreement over the character, the aims, and the means of achieving their objectives and aspirations, the partners sign a declaration of principles. After signing the declaration and the agreement on the planned activities, the partners proceed to the election of a temporary managing committee and the adoption of the internal regulation (statutes), providing the governance bodies (Annual General Assembly, Executive Committee, Chairman, General Secretary, Treasurer, Coordination Bureau, Sectoral Committees).
- *Communication of cooperation*
  One of the first tasks that the managing committee shall embark upon is publicizing the cooperation to other cities or other networks of cities.
- *Monitoring – evaluation of activities*
  A basic precondition for the success of the whole undertaking is the continuous follow up of activities, the review and the improvement, as necessary, of the procedures.

6.6　Conclusions

The ecosystem of city networks faces several challenges. Firstly, there is the risk of internal disengagement, where significant cities may question the value of network participation and opt for different directions. Some important cities may not see network engagement as a strategic international tool, highlighting a potential lack of clarity regarding the networks' contribution to the overall ecosystem and their complementarity with a shared vision (De la Varga Mas, 2019, p. 86). Second, sectors tied to traditional diplomacy, which have been hesitant to recognize cities as legitimate actors in the international system, may fuel skepticism toward international municipalism. This resistance from traditional diplomatic circles can hinder the acceptance of cities as influential global actors (Fernández de Losada, 2019, p. 25). Third, there is a lack of improvement in the dialogue between city networks and citizens, contributing to a democratic deficit in city diplomacy. While enhancing the sustainability and resilience of urban development is a common goal, new networks often lack plans for meaningful communication with citizens. Citizens are perceived more as beneficiaries of policies rather than as active participants in influencing how city networks are governed or how technical professionals think. City networks have the potential to be schools of democracy, providing spaces for cities to voice their opinions and values while respecting diverse viewpoints (Canals, 2019, p. 95). Fourth, there is a tendency to prioritize large cities in international partnerships, overlooking opportunities to invest in technologies that could significantly benefit small- and medium-sized cities. This preference for large cities may hinder the development of alliances and fail to appreciate the diversity of human settlement typologies (Allegretti, 2019, p. 46). Fifth, the substantial increase in the number and variety of city networks and platforms, particularly in the last 15 years, has led to a blurring of each network's mission, aims, and unique outputs (Cardama, 2019, p. 50). The low coordination among networks, a lack of a shared narrative, and dispersed activities around crucial cross-cutting issues reduce overall impact and may cause confusion among targeted national or international interlocutors. Addressing these challenges is crucial for city networks to realize their potential as effective platforms for global cooperation and problem-solving.

References

Aall, C., Groven, K., and Lindseth, G. (2007) "The Scope of Action for Local Climate Policy: The Case of Norway", *Global Environmental Politics*, 7 (2), pp. 83–101.

Abdullah, H., and Garcia-Chueca, E. (2020) "Cacophony or Complementarity? The Expanding Ecosystem of City Networks under Scrutiny". In S. Amiri and E. Sevin (Eds.) *City Diplomacy. Current Trends and Future Prospects* (pp. 37–58). Basingstoke: Palgrave Macmillan.

Acuto, M. (2020) "Prologue: A New Generation of City Diplomacy". In S.A.-E. Sevin (Ed.) *City Diplomacy. Current Trends and Future Prospects* (pp. vii–xi). Basingstoke: Palgrave Macmillan.

Acuto, M., Hartley, K., and Kosovac, A. (2021) "City Diplomacy: Another Generational Shift?", *Diplomatica*, 3 (1), pp. 137–146.

Acuto, M., Morissette, M., and Tsouros, A. (2017) "City Diplomacy: Towards More Strategic Networking? Learning with WHO Healthy Cities", *Global Policy*, 8 (1), pp. 14–21.

Acuto, M., and Rayner, S. (2016) "City Networks: Breaking Gridlocks or Forging (New) Lock-ins?", *International Affairs*, 92 (5), pp. 1147–1166.

Allegretti, G. (2019) "Cities and Citizens and Demodiversity: An Overview of Two Generations of Cities Networks". In A. Fernández de Losada and H. Abdullah (Eds.) *Rethinking the Ecosystem of International City Networks: Challenges and Opportunities* (pp. 39–48). Barcelona: CIDOB (Barcelona Centre for International Affairs).

Balbim, R. (2016) "City Diplomacy: Global Agendas, Local Agreements". In R. Balbim (Ed.) *The Geopolitics of Cities. Old Challenges, New Issues* (pp. 123–170). Brasilia: IPEA.

Balbim, R. (2021) "International City's Networks and Diplomacy", *Discussion Paper*, Rio de Janeiro: IPEA.

Bansard, J.S., Pattberg, P.H., and Widerberg, O. (2016) "Cities to the Rescue? Assessing the Performance of Transnational Municipal Networks in Global Climate Governance", *International Environmental Agreements: Politics, Law and Economics*, 17, pp. 229–246.

Barber, S. (1997) "International, Local and Regional Government Alliances", *Public Money & Management*, 17 (4), pp. 19–23.

Benington, J., and Harvey, J. (1994) "Spheres or Tiers? The Significance of Transnational Local Authority Networks", *Local Government Policy Making*, 20 (5), pp. 21–30.

Boix, R. (2003) "Networks of Cities and Growth: Theory, Network Identification and Measurement of the Network Externality", *European Business Module*, Firenze: Università di Firenze.

Bouteligier, S. (2013) *Cities, Networks, and Global Environmental Governance. Spaces of Innovation, Places of Leadership*, New York and London: Routledge.

Busch, H. (2015) "Linked for Action? An Analysis of Transnational Municipal Climate Networks in Germany", *International Journal of Urban Sustainable Development*, 7(2), pp. 213–231.

Camagni, R., and Salone, C. (1993) "Network Urban Structures in Northern Italy: Elements for a Theoretical Framework", *Urban Studies*, 30 (6), pp. 1053–1064.

Camps, A.G. (2019) "A View from Madrid City Council". In A. Fernández de Losada and H. Abdullah (Eds.) *Rethinking the Ecosystem of International City Networks* (pp. 79–81). Barcelona: Cidob Edicions.

Canals, M. (2019) "City Networks, An Opportunity to Learn and Share Knowledge and Know-How". In A. Fernández de Losada and H. Abdullah (Eds.) *Rethinking the Ecosystem of International City Networks* (pp. 93–96). Barcelona: CIDOB (Barcelona Centre for International Affairs).

Cardama, M. (2019) "The Emergence of New City Platforms on the International Stage: The Imperative of Reconfiguring the Ecosystem of Networks". In A. Fernández de Losada and H. Abdullah (Eds.) *Rethinking the Ecosystem of International City Networks* (pp. 49–56). Barcelona: CIDOB (Barcelona Centre for International Affairs).

Curtis, S. (2014) "The Meaning of Global Cities". In S. Curtis (Ed.) *The Power of Cities in International Relations* (pp. 16–31). London and New York: Routledge.

Curtis, S. (2016) "Introduction". In S. Curtis (Ed.) *The Power of Cities in International Relations* (pp. 1–15). London and New York: Routledge.

Curtis, S. and Acuto, M. (2018) "The Foreign Policy of Cities", *RUSI Journal*, 163 (6), pp. 8–17.

De la Varga Mas, O. (2019) "Entangled: A Reflection on the Current State of the Ecosystem of Local Government Networks". In A. Fernández de Losada and H. Abdullah (Eds.) *Rethinking the Ecosystem of International City Networks* (pp. 85–88). Barcelona: Cidob Edicions.

De Leeuw, E. (2001) "Global and Local (Glocal) Health: The WHO Healthy Cities Programme", *Global Change & Human Health*, 2, pp. 34–45. https://doi.org/10.1023/A:1011991014805.

Dematteis, G. (1994) "Global Networks, Local Cities", *Flux*, 15, pp. 17–23.

Dematteis, G., and Guarrasi, V. (Eds.) (1995) *Urban Networks*, Bologna: Patron.

Ercole, E., Walters, M., and Goldsmith, M.J.F. (1997) "Cities, Networks, Euregions, European Offices". In M.J.F. Goldsmith and K.K. Klausen (Eds.) *European Integration and Local Government* (pp. 219–236). Cheltenham & Brookfield: Edward Elgar.

Fernández de Losada, A. (2019) "Towards a Cooperative Ecosystem of City Networks". In A. Fernández de Losada and H. Abdullah (Eds.) *Rethinking the Ecosystem of International City Networks* (pp. 19–29). Barcelona: Cidob Edicions.

Giest, S., and Howlett, M. (2013) "Comparative Climate Change Governance: Lessons from European Transnational Municipal Network Management Efforts", *Environmental Policy and Governance*, 23 (6), pp. 341–353.

John, P. (1994) "The Presence and Influence of United Kingdom Local Authorities in Brussels". In P. Dunleavy & J. Stanyer (Eds.) *Contemporary Political Studies*, Vol. 2 (pp. 906–921). Belfast: Political Studies Association.

Karvounis, A. (2011) "The Europeanization of the Local Government in the EU Multi-Level Governance System: The City Networking Paradigm and the Greek Case". In E. Van Bever, H. Reynaert and K. Steyvers (Eds.) *The Road to Europe. Main Street or Backward Alley for Local Governments in Europe?* (pp. 211–231). Brugge: Vanden Broele.

Karvounis, A. (2023) *City Diplomacy and the Europeanisation of Local Government. The Prospects of Networking in the Greek Municipalities*, Cham: Palgrave Macmillan.

Keiner, M., and Kim, A. (2007) "Transnational City Networks for Sustainability", *European Planning Studies*, 15 (10), pp. 1369–1395.

Kern, K. (2007) "When Europe Hits City Hall: The Europeanization of Cities in the EU Multilevel-level System", *Biennial Conference of the European Studies Association*, 17–19 May.

Kern, K., and Bulkeley, H. (2009) "Cities, Europeanisation and Multi-Level Governance: Governing Climate Change through Transnational Municipal Networks", *Journal of Common Market Studies*, 47 (2), pp. 309–332.

Klaus, I., and Curtis, S. (2020) "Ties That Bind: China's BRI and City Diplomacy in a Shifting World Order", *Italian Institute for International Political Studies*. 6 July, [Online], URL: https://www.ispionline.it/en/pubblicazione/ties-bind-chinas-bri-and-city-diplomacy-shifting-world-order-26852.

Kosovac, A., Hartley, K., Acuto, M., and Gunning, D. (2020) *Conducting City Diplomacy. A Survey of International Engagement in 47 Cities*, Chicago-Parkville: The Chicago Council on Global Affairs & Connected Cities Lab.

Labaeye, A., and Sauer, T. (2013) "City Networks and the Socio-Ecological Transition. A European Inventory", *Work Package 501. MS89 Research Paper on Meta Study Completed, Task 501.1'. Working Paper no 27* (https://ideas.repec.org/b/wfo/wstudy/46888.html).

Lara, R. (2020) "How Are Cities Inserting Themselves in the International System?". In S. Amiri and E. Sevin (Eds.) *City Diplomacy. Current Trends and Future Prospects* (pp. 189–214). Basingstoke: Palgrave Macmillan.

Lawrence, R. (2000) "Battling for the Regions: Local Government Policy Networks and the Reform of the European Structural Funds", *Local Government Studies*, 26 (4), pp. 58–70.

Leffe, B., and Acuto, M. (2017) "City Diplomacy in the Age of Brexit and Trump", *Public Diplomacy Magazine*, Summer/Fall, 18, pp. 9–14.

Malé, J.-P. (2019) "The Emergence of City Alliances and Fronts: Towards New Forms of Local Government Influence?". In A. Fernández de Losada and H. Abdullah (Eds.) *Rethinking the Ecosystem of International City Networks* (pp. 31–37). Barcelona: Cidob Edicions.

Mush, A. (2008) *City Diplomacy: The Roles of Local Government in Peace-Building and Post-Conflict Reconstruction*, Den Haag: VNG International.

Payre, R. (2010) "The Importance of Being Connected. City Networks and Urban Government: Lyon and Eurocities (1990–2005)", *International Journal of Urban and Regional Research*, 34 (2), pp. 260–280.

Pejic, D., Acuto, M., and Kosovac, A. (2022) *City Diplomacy during COVID-19: The 2022 Cities and International Engagement Survey*, Melbourne Centre for Cities; Chicago Council on Global Affairs. https://doi.org/10.26188/19719676.

Phelps, N.A., McNeil, D., and Parsons, N. (2002) "In Search of a European Edge Urban Identity: Trans-European Networking among Edge Urban Municipalities", *European Urban and Regional Studies*, 9 (3), pp. 211–224.

Pipa, A.F., and Bouchet, M. (2021) "Partnership among cities, states, and the federal government: Creating an office of sub-national diplomacy at the US Department of State", *Brookings*. https://policycommons.net/artifacts/4144970/partnership-among-cities-states-and-federal-government/4953830/.

Rizzo, L.S. (2002) "Monitoring Analysis: City-Networks in the Euroregion (Involving Local Authorities)", *Conference of Urban and Territorial European Policies: Levels of Territorial Government*, Turin, 18–20 April.

Roca, F. (2019) "Networks of Cities or Networked Cities? Eight Theses". In A. Fernández de Losada and H. Abdullah (Eds.) *Rethinking the Ecosystem of International City Networks* (pp. 67–69). Barcelona: Cidob Edicions.

Salskov-Iversen, D. (2006a) "Global Interconnectedness – The Case of Danish Local Government". In H.K. Hansen and J. Hoff (Eds.) *Digital Governance: Networked Societies – Creating Authority, Community and Identity in a Globalized World* (pp. 141–170). Frederiksberg: Samfundslitteratur Press.

Salskov-Iversen, D. (2006b) "Learning across Borders: The Case of Danish Local Government", *International Journal of Public Sector Management*, 19 (7), pp. 673–686.

Tavares, R. (2016) *Paradiplomacy – Cities and States as Global Players*, New York: Oxford University Press.

Trullén, J., and Boix, R. (2003) "Barcelona. Metropolis policentrica en red", *Working Paper wpdea0303*, Department of Applied Economics at Universitat Autonoma of Barcelona.

7 City Branding

7.1 Introduction

Since the 1990s, the practice of place branding has emerged in cities all over the world, strengthening the connection between the cultural and the economic dimensions of city diplomacy. This approach stems from the widely accepted assumption that "future competition between nations, cities, and enterprises looks set to be based less on natural resources, location or past reputation and more on the ability to develop attractive images and symbols and project these effectively" (Landry and Bianchini, 1995, p. 12), in accordance with a city's ability to influence behavior of other nations or cities through city diplomacy's soft power rather than coercion and force (Nye, 1990). The close relationship of city diplomacy and city branding has already been stressed in the relevant literature; still, the shared territory of the commonalities is understudied. In this sense, this chapter discusses the relevancy of the concepts in the recent literature and places emphasis on their synergies in cultural and economic domains. The chapter is divided into four sections. The first one introduces the terminology coined and used in the literature on city branding. The second identifies the relationship of city branding with the soft power of city diplomacy. The third section, building upon the previous discussions, presents the main synergies between them in the cultural and economic domains. Finally, the fourth section links city branding activities with the internationalization strategy of the local authorities and underlines the main conditions for enhancing city's international distinctiveness.

7.2 The Concept of City Branding

In today's competitive and marketing savvy world, branding is accepted as a fundamental strategy for competitive advantage and success. And cities, like companies, are beginning to use branding to help them market themselves for investment, tourism, and exports. Yet, unlike nation branding, which has attracted scholarly attention, city branding is a more recent domain of academic enquiry (de Andrade and dos Santos, 2021, pp. 105–125).

DOI: 10.4324/9781003470908-10

Specifically, the urban perspective gained traction in the 1990s in conjunction with the tourism marketing perspective (Ashworth and Voogd, 1990, 1994b), with titles such as "city marketing" (Ashworth and Voogd, 1994a) and "city selling" (Ward, 1998). The first attempts to link "branding" to cities were made in the 2000s, when place product branding was replaced with place branding, which increases preference, distinction, and loyalty (Hankinson, 2010, pp. 15–17). The importance of branding to cities was underlined by Hankinson (2001, pp. 132–136) from the product branding approach. According to Greenberg (2000, p. 256), the urban lifestyle promoted by periodicals under the quality of life concept contained branded cities in miniature. Evans (2003, pp. 420–421) examined the role that cultural brands have in providing a feeling of distinction and community inside cities. Rainisto (2003, p. 63) emphasized the necessity of adapting branding principles to specific locations. Notably, studies about municipal branding increased exponentially between 1998 and 2009 (Lucarelli and Berg, 2011, p. 11). Then, Kavaratzis (2004, pp. 63–67) offered a framework to examine city brand and management in the first issue of "Place Branding and Public Diplomacy". This framework consists of five components that are based on the corporate branding approach: (1) landscape; (2) infrastructure projects; (3) organizational structure; (4) city behavior; and (5) intentional communication.

The author made it clear that corporate brands refer to a collection of distinct brands that together enhance a company's reputation. Rather than focusing on the specific strategies of product branding, this viewpoint takes a larger, more comprehensive approach to brand development (Kavaratzis, 2020, p. 25). Actually, that paper paved the way for the groundbreaking study co-authored by Kavaratzis and Ashworth (2006), which is regarded as classical (Hospers, 2020, p. 18) and served as the impetus for the *Tijdschrift voor Economische en Sociale Geografe's* special issue titled "Revisiting City Branding", which was published in February 2020 (Kavaratzis, 2020). Kavaratzis and Ashworth (2006, pp. 189–191) created the concept of "responsible city branding" in that study, which was backed by corporate branding. Regarding this, Kavaratzis (2019, p. 1) pointed out that city branding is the application of branding philosophy and methods to city development, with two associated outcomes: (1) gaining a competitive edge, boosting investments and tourism; and (2) promoting social inclusion and development.

Anholt (2006b, pp. 18–20) argued that city branding consists of a few characteristics, a pledge, and a narrative that influences the choice to travel to the city, purchase its goods and services, conduct business there, or even relocate. The elements that make up the city brand hexagon are as follows: (1) presence: the city's reputation abroad; (2) place: people's perceptions; (3) potential: commercial and educational prospects; (4) pulse: a dynamic way of life; (5) people: the friendliness and safety of the locals; and (6) prerequisites: the fundamental characteristics of the city. Later, Anholt (2007, pp. 3, 59–62) renamed the concept to "competitive identity", a term he used to describe synthesis of brand management with public diplomacy and with trade, investment, tourism, and export promotion. Nevertheless, the cities' hexagon remained the same.

This short review of the existing literature suggests there are recurring arguments that resonate across the city branding research corpus. First, a city's brand begins with a certain *image*. According to Kavaratzis and Ashworth (2006) and Herstein (2012), the branding of a city is therefore a "planned practice of signification and representation". For instance, to dispel the notion that Bogota is just "another South American poor mega-city, devastated by crime and drugs", the city submitted a bid for a city branding campaign in 2009 (Kalandides, 2011). Negative representations of Bogota in the media and popular culture are to blame for the spread of this image. Second, financial gain is frequently the driving force behind city branding (Kotler and Gertner, 2002; Middleton, 2011). Cities have a distinct identity that makes them stand out in a globalized world where they compete with one another for investments, visitors, and job opportunities (Caldwell and Freire, 2004).

In the early 2000s, Amsterdam had to start a city branding effort because of the growing drug competition and the city's red-light district, which was turning away wealthy visitors. Thus, Amsterdam made the decision to set itself apart by associating itself with three new fundamental values: inventiveness, creativity, and the spirit of trade (Kavaratzis and Ashworth, 2006). The fact that "everything a city consists of, everything that takes place in a city and is done by the city, communicates messages about the city's brand" (Kavaratzis, 2009) further complicates city branding. Mega-events can be crucial to a city's branding since they garner extensive media coverage and have the potential to alter the city's physical environment through architectural and infrastructural upgrades. Beijing underwent significant landscape modifications in preparation for hosting the 2008 Olympic Games, as the city's authorities aimed to position Beijing as an eco-friendly global city that embraces both modernity and history. But Beijing's deplorable environmental state, its deteriorating infrastructure, and China's contempt for human rights all directly contradicted Beijing's new image and kept it from becoming widely recognized (Zhang and Zhao, 2009). Lastly, culture and art are major components of city branding (Kavaratzis, 2009). One way to launch cultural branding is to organize large-scale events or set up new cultural establishments, such as Bilbao's Guggenheim. A city's image can also be changed by its culture. For example, after the city's automotive industry declined, Turin initiated a city branding campaign to associate the city with innovation and the arts (Vanolo, 2008).

Given the core elements of city branding and the foundational goal of city diplomacy – focused on promoting trade, policies, and the global image, fostering positive relations through cooperation, collaboration, cultural ties, civic exchanges, and goodwill – it's unsurprising that existing literature highlights a close connection between public diplomacy, managed by city governments, and place branding (Anholt, 2002, pp. 230–231), as the following section will make more clear.

7.3   The Relevancy of City Branding for City Diplomacy

In this section, from the branding side, contributions mentioned below addressing nations and places (cities and regions) have used terms often interchangeably (Papadopoulos, 2004, pp. 36–37). Anholt (2006a) wrote about nation branding even though he meant to talk about the connection between public diplomacy and place branding. Fan, the guest editor of the "Place Branding and Public Diplomacy" special issue on city branding, stressed the significance of city branding for cities' futures (Fan, 2014, pp. 253–254). Comparable studies have been conducted on the relevance of catchy titles (Dudek-Mánkowska and Grochowski, 2019) and the influence of local governments on nation branding (Wang, 2006, pp. 32–34). The shared goals of Chinese public diplomacy at the national level and Ningbo branding at the local level were investigated in a recent research (Zhang et al., 2020). In fact, Wang (2006, p. 32) stated that public diplomacy corresponds with the "culture element" of the "Nation Brands Hexagon" and is a means of fostering reputation and image through the dissemination of policies and culture to global publics. According to Anholt (2007, p. 60), this relates to the "presence element" of the "City Brands Hexagon". Anholt (2002, pp. 230–231) emphasized the necessity of coordinating branding strategies with diplomatic efforts and stated that the concept of a competitive identity is derived from public diplomacy combined with brand management.

Similarly, Melissen (2005, pp. 19–21) called them "sisters under the skin" due to their shared objective of bringing ideas to foreign audiences and their reliance on listening to improve outcomes from long-term strategies. He does, however, make a distinction between place branding and public diplomacy, noting that the latter is more concerned with identity projection and the former is more focused on international relations. Melissen (2005, pp. 20–21) cautiously has noted that, despite being directed at international audiences, branding and diplomacy have a crucially essential domestic reference, which can weaken each other when working on opposing viewpoints.

According to Pamment et al. (2017, p. 326), both support nation states' communication management strategies aimed at luring in trade, investment, and tourists as well as generating interest in their policies and values on a larger scale. Szondi (2008, p. 14) conducted a thorough analysis of the parallels and divergences between nation branding and public diplomacy. The latter is interpreted as a place branding speciality that enables transferability to other cities. Five different relationships were mapped in this scenario: (1) unrelation; (2) public diplomacy as part of branding; (3) branding as part of public diplomacy; (4) exactly same concepts; and (5) partial overlapping. Szondi concluded by saying that combining the two ideas will result in synergy.

For instance, China has been successful in using branding and city diplomacy. China has adopted city branding approaches to stimulate growth in major cities and facilitate urbanization. As a matter of fact, Guangzhou has been branded at the national, regional, and municipal levels as a "hub city" or "an international hub for air travel, air cargo and technology innovation, with a heavy focus on high-end and high-quality modern industrial system" (Ye and Björner, 2009). As is the case with other nations, China also uses city branding practices to enable its major cities to compete in a global marketplace against other mega-cities. In North America, the Massachusetts Office of Travel and Tourism contracts with destination marketing agencies in its six primary markets (UK, Germany, Japan, France, Italy, and Ireland) to implement comprehensive promotional programs. Marketing and public relations activities include, but are not limited to, ongoing proactive travel trade outreach, international travel trade and consumer shows, destination training programs, cooperative marketing with in-market travel partners, familiarization tours, media relations, and consumer promotions (Tavares, 2016).

To sum up, scholars identified differences, but recognize the equal importance of public diplomacy and branding to advance policies of places. This analysis can be transferred to cities' context by melting city branding and diplomacy in order to get the following synergies between the two concepts in the cultural and economic domains.

7.3.1 City Branding as a Pillar for Cultural City Diplomacy

City branding often focuses on culture and art (Kavaratzis, 2009). Kunzmann (2004) argues that in the global age, local identity has become a key concern and the arts are the last bastion of local identity. It is not thus uncommon for city diplomacy efforts to leverage the uniqueness of specific cultures or heritage to achieve international interest on global platforms. According to the Global Power City Index in 2022, London has been ranked as the most comprehensively powerful city in the world, outperforming New York, Tokyo, Paris, Singapore, and Amsterdam. London tops the ranking for Tourist Attractions and remains at the top in the cultural interaction function (GPCI, 2022). In 2006 the High Museum of Art in Atlanta loaned hundreds of works from the Louvre's collections through a 3-year partnership program. This partnership allowed Atlanta to build its reputation as a cultural center and promote its brand abroad. In 2015, Tunisia and Italy engaged in a cultural exchange with the aim of using culture to promote peaceful conflict resolution and transnational cooperation. The move followed the terrorist attack targeting Tunis' Bardo National Museum, which claimed 23 lives including four Italian nationals in March. In October, *La Republica* reported that the cities of Turin and Tunis had signed a far-reaching agreement including the economic and cultural sectors, as well as universities, urban policies, energy, water, transport, and waste. Details of the cultural aspect of the deal included loans and joint exhibitions between the Bardo Museum and Turin's Museo di Arte Orientale. Turin mayor Piero Fassino hailed the agreement as "a cooperation that should be seen as a contribution to peace and stability in the Mediterranean". In early December 2015, Bardo had loaned several pieces from its collection to the National Archaeological Museum in Aquileia, Italy, which is a UNESCO World Heritage Site. The exhibition – which was on view until 31 January 2016 – focused on the historic links and artistic influences between North Africa and Italy. "The best response to what is happening is not just military solutions, but also and above all the cultural route", Debora Serracchiani, governor of the Friuli-Venezia Giulia region, made clear (Neuendorf, 2015). In this way, museums as central hubs of international collaborations have not just earned cities a reputation of the global cultural destination, but also provide soft power resources to complement city diplomacy in a more sustained and long-term manner. The role of museums as facilitators of city diplomacy initiatives became more evident on 14 October 2015 when Mayor of Turin and the Minister of Palestinian Local Government, Hussein Al Araj, signed a Cooperation Agreement between the Municipality of Bethlehem and the City of Turin, to support local development in the management of water and trade resources. The event took place at the Museum of Oriental Art that for this occasion opened a dedicated exhibition on historical objects coming from Palestine (City of Torino, 2016).

7.3.2   City Branding as a Catalyst for Economic City Diplomacy

In parallel with cultural goals, city branding plays a crucial role in the economic dimension of city diplomacy, particularly in today's highly integrated global economy. Marketing and place branding, integral to economic promotion in city diplomacy, have become increasingly central (Kotler et al., 1993). Cities pursue economic interests through pull activities, attracting capital by drawing tourists, hosting global institutions, and organizing major events, such as fairs and sports competitions. Pull activities, notably city branding, apply business marketing techniques to promote a city as a brand, exemplified by slogans, such as "I Love NY". Successful examples include Amsterdam, Berlin, and Copenhagen, showcasing well-executed marketing campaigns that enhance their international appeal. Constructing a city narrative shapes a public image, generating soft power and influencing political processes at national and international levels.

Hosting global events is a significant component of the international political projection of cities. Although the organization of global events has an important economic dimension, it has also public relations impact (Marchetti, 2021). Major events, such as the Olympic Games, FIFA World Cups, and World Expos have significant impacts on the soft power, perceptions, and international reputations of host cities (Long, 2022). The economic benefits include immediate stimulus, long-term economic gains, new infrastructures, and security force training. Non-economic benefits involve favorable publicity, enhanced global engagement, and improved international image.

These events contribute to city development and influence on the global agenda (Kirton et al., 2010). The preparatory phases, collectively termed "mega-event strategy", involve coordinated efforts of mayors, local governments, public administration, and businesses. Since the inception of the Olympic Games in 1896, host cities have used the games to project a specific image of themselves to the world. Barcelona was no different. The 1992 Olympic Games in Barcelona exemplified a successful city-branding strategy, elevating the city's international image and tourism appeal.[1]

Conversely, hosting international summits are not risk free and may also laden hosts with considerable costs, ongoing debt, and negative publicity. This explains why some mayors are reluctant to bid for the Olympics and other high-profile events. For example, the Athens Olympics left lasting financial burdens, challenging the romanticized notion associated with hosting. Available stats showed that the Athens Olympics increased tourism in Italy – people looking for Mediterranean sun tried to avoid Greece, went to Italy instead. Furthermore, an economic analysis of hosting sports mega-events has found "very little positive effect" on tourism from three football World Cups and five Olympic Games. The Olympics wouldn't have bankrupted Greece, but they certainly didn't help (Reynolds, 2015).

All in all, city hosting an international mega-event or summit is not just a passive space controlled by sovereign actors; it actively engages in diplomatic dialogue with other cities to tackle global challenges. Cities, beyond collective action, can assume leadership in addressing global issues to bolster their standing in national and international governance. However, achieving this necessitates a collaborative strategy to enhance their international image (Le Gales, 2002).

7.4 City Branding and the Internationalization Strategy

City branding is closely tied to a broader strategy for internationalization (see Chapter 9), where the city mayor plays a key role in developing a strategic document focused on urban planning for international distinctiveness. In the global competition for economic and cultural success, cities strategically differentiate themselves while collaborating in networks, such as C40 cities and European Metropolitan Authorities to enhance attractiveness, visibility, and influence (Asdourian and Ingenhoff, 2020). Buenos Aires serves as an illustrative example, having established a General Secretariat for International Relations to coordinate its international activities and developed a comprehensive strategy for global projection. Strategy's objectives include attracting visitors, students, and economic activities, recognizing the city's potential among global players. The strategy emphasizes identity, reputation, and visibility, aiming to position Buenos Aires as a global capital with a high quality of life. Culture, a significant component, is promoted through UNESCO

Creative Cities Network, fostering creativity in local industries with projects, such as the Design District and Bienal Arte Joven, contributing to contemporary city branding.

City branding and internationalization strategy rely on cities' soft power, demanding a delicate balance of political, economic, and cultural elements. The secret of success is crafting a unique, inspiring narrative. City managers must skillfully align diverse urban forces for international unity, creating a shared workspace for varied entities engaging diverse audiences – a notable organizational challenge. Collaboration with local stakeholders pivotal to the city's global dimension is imperative, with no viable alternative. For example, Utrecht approaches city branding through a coalition-based, horizontal process, involving a select group of key entities. Zurich formalizes cooperation with a city, Canton of Zurich, Zurich Tourism, and the Greater Zurich Area, responsible for inward investment attraction. Johannesburg's External Relations Unit oversees international development, divided into sections handling tasks, such as town-twinning programs and supporting government offices. Johannesburg's strategy aims to boost city visibility while positioning it as a gateway to the rest of Africa (Mbinza, 2023).

Although there is no one single formula to institutionalize city branding in the framework of a collaborative internationalization strategy of a local authority, a number of key elements should be taken into account in any case:

- Partnership: The challenge is moving from participation to promoting clearer assignments for those that interact regularly with international targets (who should do what), based on accountability.
- Leadership: From the negotiation to clarify roles to the process of minimizing the potential conflict that is inherent to city brand building and governance, a roadmap and a leadership are needed. Moreover, city branding is about increasing efficiency and changing behaviors and old ways of doing things if necessary. And that needs leadership and clear political backing.
- Dedicated team: Launching, monitoring and keeping current an international city brand strategy require for full-time professionals with the right profile. A small team with a dear mandate can be enough, even for big cities.
- Effective local inter-department cooperation: Some dose of awareness and capacity building among city officers about the role of strategic communication and marketing for the city can be helpful. This is what Gothenburg's communications manager Anton Cesar calls "branding from inside-out".
- Funding model: Learning on how to promote the city internationally with small budgets is necessary as well as breaking the vicious circle of "no money no action" in which some local governments are usually trapped.
- Transnational alliances for co-branding: For instance, further to the Oresund overall cooperation, Copenhagen is actively trying to present the

whole Swedish region around Malmö as part of its hinterland for international city marketing purposes. A number of capitals, such as Helsinki, Hamburg, Riga, Stockholm, Warsaw, and St. Petersburg have explored how to pool resources for jointly branding and marketing the Baltic Sea Region, in the framework of the ONE BSR project (Grandi, 2020).

7.5 Conclusions

Competition and collaboration are the key components of the main overlapping synergies of city diplomacy and city branding. As cities compete internationally for success in various policy domains, they do so acting collaboratively, using city branding to attract international visibility to their efforts. In this sense, this chapter analyzed the intersection of city diplomacy and city branding, focusing on their connectivities in the cultural and economic domains, and positioning city branding within the city internationalization strategy. City branding is not just a dimension of city diplomacy; it provides the international aims of the local authority with a path into the future. In this sense, a crucial element for a local authority in its endeavor to earn an international reputation adopting city branding perspective, either hosting mega-events, such as Olympic Games or World Expos, or making use of facilitators, such as museums, is a collaborative internationalization strategy, which requires partnerships, leadership, dedicated team, inter-department cooperation, a funding model, and transnational alliances.

Note

1 https://www.barcelonaglobal.org/blog/en/barcelona-city-of-talent/30-anos-desde-los-juegos-olimplicos-que-cambiaron-barcelona/.

References

Anholt, S. (2002) "Foreword", *Journal of Brand Management*, 9 (4–5), pp. 229–239.
Anholt, S. (2006a) "Public Diplomacy and Place Branding: Where's the Link?", *Place Branding and Public Diplomacy*, 2 (4), pp. 271–275.
Anholt, S. (2006b) "The Anholt-GMI City Brand Index: How the World Sees the World's Cities", *Place Branding and Public Diplomacy*, 2 (1), pp. 18–23.
Anholt, S. (2007) *Competitive Identity: The New Brand Management for Nations, Cities and Regions*, London: Palgrave.
Asdourian, B., and Ingenhoff, D. (2020) "A Framework of City Diplomacy on Positive Outcomes and Negative Emotional Engagement: How to Enhance the International Role of Cities and City/Mayor Branding on Twitter?". In S. Amiri and E. Sevin (Eds.) *City Diplomacy. Current Trends and Future Prospects*. Cham: Palgrave Macmillan.
Ashworth, G.J., and Voogd, J.H. (1990) *Selling the City: Marketing Approaches in Public Sector Urban Planning*, London: Belhaven.

Ashworth, G.J., and Voogd, J.H. (1994a) "Marketing and Place Promotion". In J.R. Gold and S.V. Ward (Eds.) *Place Promotion: The Use of Publicity and Marketing to Sell Towns and Regions.* Chechester: Wiley.

Ashworth, G.J., and Voogd, J.H. (1994b) "Marketing of Tourism Places: What Are We Doing?", *Journal of International Consumer Marketing*, 6 (3–4), pp. 5–19.

Caldwell, N., and Freire, J.R. (2004) "The Differences between Branding a Country, a Region and a City: Applying the Brand Box Model", *Journal of Brand Management*, 12 (1), pp. 50–61.

City of Torino (2016) *Annual Report 2015 – International Activities of the City of Torino*, City of Torino: International Affairs, European Projects, Cooperation and Peace Service [Online], URL: http://www.comune.torino.it/relint/inglese/bm~doc/annual-report-2015_web.pdf.

De Andrade, N., and Dos Santos, S.F. (2021) "Crossroads between City Diplomacy and City Branding towards the Future: Case Study on the Film Cities at UNESCO Creative Cities Network", *Place Branding and Public Diplomacy*, 17, pp. 105–125.

Dudek-Mánkowska, S., and Grochowski, M. (2019) "From Creative Industries to the Creative Place Brand: Some Reflections on City Branding in Poland", *Place Branding and Public Diplomacy*, 15 (4), pp. 274–287.

Evans, G. (2003) "Hard-Branding the Cultural City: From Prado to Prada", *International Journal of Urban and Regional Research*, 27 (2), pp. 417–440.

Fan, H. (2014) "Foreword", *Place Branding and Public Diplomacy*, 10 (4), pp. 53–25.

GPCI (2022) *Global Power City Index 2022*, Tokyo: The Mori Memorial Foundation.

Grandi, L.K. (2020) *City Diplomacy*, Cham: Palgrave Macmillan.

Greenberg, M. (2000) "Branding Cities: A Social History of the Urban Lifestyle Magazine", *Urban Affairs Review*, 36 (2), pp. 228–263.

Hankinson, G. (2001) "Location Branding: A Study of the Branding Practices of 12 English Cities", *Journal of Brand Management*, 9 (2), pp. 127–142.

Hankinson, G. (2010) "Place Branding Theory: A Cross-Domain Literature Review from a Marketing Perspective". In G. Ashworth and M. Kavaratzis (Eds.) *Towards Effective Place Brand Management: Branding European Cities and Regions.* Cheltenham: Edward Elgar.

Herstein, R. (2012) "Thin Line between Country, City and Region Branding", *Journal of Vacation Marketing*, 18 (2), pp. 147–155.

Hospers, G.-J. (2020) "A Short Refection on City Branding and Its Controversies", *Tijdschrift voor Economische en Sociale Geografe*, 111 (1), pp. 18–23. https://doi.org/10.1111/tesg.12386.

Kalandides, A. (2011) "City Marketing for Bogota: A Case Study in Integrated Place Branding", *Journal of Place Management and Development*, 4 (3), pp. 282–291.

Kavaratzis, M. (2004) "From City Marketing to City Branding: Towards a Theoretical Framework for Developing City Brands", *Place Branding and Public Diplomacy*, 1 (1), pp. 58–73.

Kavaratzis, M. (2009) "Cities and Their Brands: Lessons from Corporate Branding", *Place Branding and Public Diplomacy*, 5 (1), pp. 26–37.

Kavaratzis, M. (2019) "City Branding". In A. Orum (Ed.) *The Wiley Blackwell Encyclopedia of Urban and Regional Studies*. https://doi.org/10.1002/9781118568446. eurs0046.

Kavaratzis, M. (2020) "Is 'city branding' Worth Re-Visiting?", *Tijdschrift voor Economische en Sociale Geografe*, 111 (1), pp. 24–27. https://doi.org/10.1111/tesg.12403.

Kavaratzis, M., and Ashworth, G.J. (2006) "City Branding: An Effective Assertion of Identity or a Transitory Marketing Trick?", *Place Branding and Public Diplomacy*, 2 (3), pp. 183–194.

Kirton, J., Guebert, J., and Tanna, S. (2010) *G8 and G20 Summit Costs*, U.o.T. Munk School for Global Affairs, Trans. Toronto: G8 and G20 Research Groups.

Kotler, P.D., and Gertner, D. (2002) "Country as Brand, Product, and Beyond: A Place Marketing and Brand Management Perspective", *Journal of Brand Management*, 9 (4), pp. 249–261.

Kotler, P.D., Haider, H., and Rein, I. (1993) *Marketing of Places*, New York: Free Press.

Kunzmann, K. (2004) "Culture, Creativity and Spatial Planning", *Town Planning Review*, 75 (4), pp. 383–404.

Landry, C., and Bianchini, F. (1995) *The Creative City*, London: Demos.

Le Gales, P. (2002) *European Cities: Social Conflicts and Governance*, New York: Oxford University Press.

Long, Z. (2022) "Documentary series shows Shanghai's charm at Dubai World Expo". https://www.shine.cn/news/world/2202232279/.

Lucarelli, A., and Berg, P.O. (2011) "City Branding: A State-of-the Art Review of the Research Domain", *Journal of Place Management and Development*, 14 (1), pp. 9–27.

Marchetti, R. (2021) *City Diplomacy. From City-States to Global Cities*, Ann Arbor: University of Michigan Press.

Mbinza, Z. (2023) "Exploring Place Branding in the Global South: The Case of Johannesburg, South Africa", *Place Branding and Public Diplomacy*. https://doi.org/10.1057/s41254-023-00314-5.

Melissen, J. (2005) "The New Public Diplomacy: Between Theory and Practice". In J. Melissen (Ed.) *The New Public Diplomacy: Soft Power in International Relations* (pp. 3–27). New York: Palgrave.

Middleton, A.C. (2011) "City Branding and Inward Investment". In N. Morgan, A. Pritchard and R. Pride (Eds.) *Destination Brands: Managing Place Reputation* (pp. 335–346). Oxford: Butterworth-Heinemann.

Neuendorf, H. (2015) "Tunisia's Bardo Museum enters Cultural Exchange with Italian institutions", *Artnet*. https://news.artnet.com/art-world/bardo-museum-tunis-italian-exchange-396924.

Nye, J.S. (1990) "Soft Power", *Foreign Policy*, 80, pp. 153–171.

Pamment, J., Olofsson, A., and Hjrth-Jenssen, R. (2017) "The Response of Swedish and Norwegian Public Diplomacy and Nation Branding Actors to the Refugee Crisis", *Journal of Communication Management*, 21 (4), pp. 326–341.

Papadopoulos, N. (2004) "Place Branding: Evolution, Meaning and Implications", *Place Branding Public Diplomacy*, 1 (1), pp. 36–49.

Rainisto, S. (2003) *"Success factors of place marketing: A study of place marketing practices in northern Europe and the United States"*, Doctoral Dissertation, Helsinki University of Technology, Institute of Strategy and International Business.

Reynolds, E. (2015) "A Dark Olympic Legacy for Greece", https://www.news.com.au/sport/sports-li-fe/a-dark-olympic-legacy-for-greece/newsstory/8dcf6d1e8df9fe2e0f93ff12e74b1b72.

Szondi, G. (2008) "Public diplomacy and nation branding: Conceptual similarities and differences", *Clingendael Discussion Papers in Diplomacy*, Den Haag: Netherlands Institute of International Relations 'Clingendael'.

Tavares, R. (2016) *Paradiplomacy – Cities and States as Global Players*, New York: Oxford University Press.

Vanolo, A. (2008) "The Image of the Creative City: Some Reflections on Urban Branding in Turin", *Cities*, 25 (6), pp. 370–382.

Wang, J. (2006) "Localising Public Diplomacy: The Role of Subnational Actors in Nation Branding", *Place Branding and Public Diplomacy*, 2 (1), pp. 32–42.

Ward, S.V. (1998) *Selling Places: The Marketing and Promotion of Towns and Cities 1850–2000*, London: Routledge.

Ye, L., and Björner, E. (2009) "Linking City Branding to Multi-Level Urban Governance in Chinese Mega-Cities: A Case Study of Guangzhou", *Cities*, 80, pp. 29–37.

Zhang, S.I., Wang, Y., Liu, N.X., and Loo, Y.-M. (2020) "Ningbo city branding and public diplomacy under the belt and road initiative in China", *Place Branding and Public Diplomacy*. https://doi.org/10.1057/s41254-020-00161-8.

Zhang, L., and Zhao, S.X. (2009) "City Branding and the Olympic Effect: A Case Study of Beijing", *Cities*, 26 (5), pp. 245–254.

8 Smart Cities

8.1 Introduction

Cities globally engage in smart initiatives driven by local governments aiming to provide advanced services through technology adoption. Various sectors, including waste management, energy, health, education, and public transportation, showcase digital innovation's potential to enhance living standards and attract international interest. The smart city concept, still evolving and debated, often centers on digital innovation by corporate players, such as IBM, CISCO, Intel, GE, Microsoft, Oracle, and Amazon, focusing on cloud-based platforms and solutions. Technology plays a key role in enabling new processes, transforming organizational arrangements, and shaping individual choices. Emerging technologies, such as 3D printing, IoT, big data analytics, AI, energy storage, civic tech, drones, and Blockchain, are poised to impact urban development by 2025. Autonomous vehicles (AVs) and various smart applications in security, healthcare, mobility, energy, and more are already in use. However, the smart city concept has evolved beyond its original narrow definition, causing confusion in international comparisons. Smart governance involves local administrations, public agencies, firms, citizens, and communities. Cities don't grow in isolation; they coexist, collaborate, compete, and evolve together. ICT and transport networks facilitate intensive communication among cities, enabling international cooperation. This interdependence fosters smart city diplomacy, where cities share solutions and insights to address common challenges, creating a network of knowledge exchange and collaboration. This chapter will discuss the concept of smart city as well as the various ways in which smart city and city diplomacy can be combined.

8.2 The Concept of Smart City

The term "smart city" is a fuzzy concept that is not used consistently within the literature. Indeed, "smart" is often used interchangeably with the terms "intelligent", "wired", and "digital" (Tranos and Gertner, 2012, p. 176). As a result, various forms of policy models have been developed. These include

DOI: 10.4324/9781003470908-11

the concepts of "wired cities" (Dutton, 1987), "technocities" (Downey and McGuigan, 1999), "digital cities" (Komninos, 2008), "creative cities" (Florida, 2005), and "knowledge-based cities" (Carrillo, 2006). One of the main criticisms is "the disjuncture between image and reality [...] the real difference between a city actually being intelligent, and it simply lauding a smart label" (Hollands, 2008, p. 305). This section explores the various definitions proposed by the relevant literature, national governments, and international organizations.

Hollands (2008) provides a comprehensive review on the smart city concept. Following on from Hollands, Caragliu et al. (2009) add a critical review of the literature from an economic perspective. According to these authors, actual smart cities can be seen to embody specific characteristics that include digital infrastructure and ICT usage, emphasis on business-led urban development, the social inclusion agenda via e-governance, concern with high-tech and creative industries in urban growth, the importance of social capital in urban development, and the inclusion of environmental and social sustainability (Caragliu et al., 2009; Hollands, 2008). In particular, Caragliu et al. (2009) consider that a city is smart when investments in human and social capital and traditional (transport) and modern (ICT) communication infrastructure fuel sustainable economic growth and a high quality of life, with a wise management of natural resources, through participatory governance. On his part, Hollands (2008) has argued that smart cities are "... territories with a high capacity for learning and innovation, which is built in to the creativity of their population, their institutions of knowledge production, and their digital infrastructure for communication". For the rest of the literature, the concept of smart city is more related to that of sustainability (Kourtit et al., 2012; Mahizhnan, 1999; Thuzar, 2011) and less to the diffusion of ICTs, but it also moves from and looks at "participatory governance" (Caragliu et al., 2011), "intellectual ability" (Zygiaris, 2013), "high capacity for learning and innovation" (Komninos, 2006), "metropolitan areas with adult population holding a college degree" (Winters, 2011), "creativity" (Thite, 2011), "highly educated people, knowledge-intensive jobs, output-oriented planning systems, creative activities ..." (Kourtit and Nijkamp, 2012), "smart combination of endowments and activities of self-decisive, independent and aware citizens" (Giffender et al., 2007).

The concept of smart cities is often associated with various related terms such as digital, intelligent, virtual, and ubiquitous cities. These terms represent specific and less inclusive levels of city concepts, and the smart city often encompasses and extends them. A digital city is characterized by a connected community with broadband communications infrastructure, a flexible, service-oriented computing infrastructure based on open industry standards, and innovative services for governments, citizens, and businesses. The goal is to create an environment for information sharing, collaboration, interoperability, and seamless experiences throughout the city (Ishida, 2002). The intelligent city concept emerges at the intersection of the knowledge society and the digital city. Intelligent cities consciously use information technology to fundamentally transform life and work. They support learning, technological development, and innovation processes. While every digital city may not necessarily be intelligent, every intelligent city has digital components, yet it may lack the people and community perspective included in a smart city (Komninos, 2011). The ubiquitous city extends the concept of a digital city in terms of ubiquitous accessibility and infrastructure. It leverages ubiquitous computing to make services available to urban elements. Unlike the virtual city, which visualizes urban elements, the ubiquitous city utilizes computer chips or sensors embedded in urban elements for real-time data collection and interaction. In a virtual city, city functions are implemented in a cyberspace, creating a hybrid concept with both physical and virtual elements. The virtual city reproduces urban elements by visualizing them within the virtual space, creating a parallel representation of real entities and people (Lee et al., 2013). A knowledge city is designed to encourage the nurturing of knowledge and is interchangeable to some extent with concepts, such as an educating city. It emphasizes characteristics, such as being clever, smart, skillful, creative, networked, connected, and competitive. The idea is integral to knowledge-based urban development, aligning with the broader concept of a smart city (Dirks et al., 2010). These terms represent different dimensions of urban development, each focusing on specific aspects of technology, intelligence, virtualization, ubiquity, and knowledge within the city context. The smart city concept, by incorporating these elements, aims to create comprehensive and interconnected urban environments that leverage technology for the benefit of citizens and sustainable development.

Governments and public agencies globally are adopting the idea of smart cities to distinguish their policies for sustainable development, economic growth, and citizens' well-being. The concept evolves, taking different forms and interpretations across countries. According to Organisation for Economic Cooperation and Development (OECD, 2019a, 8), in Denmark, the Ministry of Transport, Building, and Housing and the Danish Business Authority see "Smart City" as a concept extending beyond environmental and infrastructure issues. It now encompasses various areas, such as business development, innovation, citizen involvement, culture, healthcare, and social services, leveraging data and digital platforms for innovative solutions. In Korea, the Ministry of Land, Infrastructure and Transportation defines a smart city as one utilizing digitalization, clean energy, and innovative transport technologies to offer environmentally friendly choices. Smart cities are viewed as tools to solve urban problems, improve quality of life, and enhance service delivery through ICTs. In Latvia, the Ministry of Environmental Protection and Regional Development defines a smart city as implementing a strategic package of measures to address challenges, boost competitiveness, provide efficient public services, improve overall well-being, and anticipate potential issues. Smart development planning is emphasized, fostering cooperation between stakeholders. In Spain, the government aligns with the Spanish Association for Standardization and Certification, defining a smart city as a holistic approach, using ICTs to enhance inhabitants' quality of life, accessibility, and sustainable economic, social, and environmental development. It emphasizes real-time adaptation to citizens' needs and open data provision. In the United Kingdom, the Department of Business, Energy and Industrial Strategy sees the smart city concept as dynamic, lacking a static or absolute definition. It is viewed as a continual process by which cities become more livable, resilient, and responsive to new challenges over time.

At international level, according to the European Commission, a smart city is an urban area using electronic data-collection sensors to efficiently manage assets and resources. This includes data from citizens, devices, and assets for monitoring and managing various systems such as transportation, power plants, water supply, waste management, law enforcement, information systems, schools, libraries, hospitals, and community services (CEC, 2019a, p. 139). Smart cities are defined by the OECD as initiatives leveraging digitalization to enhance citizen well-being and deliver efficient, sustainable, and inclusive urban services through a collaborative, multi-stakeholder process (OECD, 2018). A smart city approach, as defined by the United Nations, is utilizing opportunities from digitalization, clean energy, and innovative transport technologies to provide environmentally friendly choices, boost sustainable economic growth, and improve service delivery (United Nations, 2016). A smart and sustainable city is defined by the Inter American Development Bank as an innovative city using ICT and other means to improve quality of life, operational efficiency, competitiveness, and meeting present and future needs in economic, social, and environmental aspects (Bouskela et al., 2016).

Finally, for United Cities and Local Government (UCLG), a smart city is one using information and communications technology to make critical infrastructure, components, and utilities more interactive and efficient, fostering citizen awareness. UCLG emphasizes a broader definition, considering a city "smart" when investments in human and social capital, communications infrastructure, and participatory governance promote sustainable economic development and a high quality of life across six areas: economy, citizens, management, mobility, environment, and quality of life (UCLG, 2012, p. 21).

As it is presented in the literature above, apart from very few exemptions (Centre of Regional Science, 2007; Komninos, 2002), the smart city concept only focuses on the local-urban scale and does not consider global urban interdependencies. Therefore, questions emerge on how a city may become a learning territory with high capacity for innovation if it is not intensively linked with the distributed centers of production and consumption and with the world recognized research sites? Put simply, how can a city become smart in the frame of the post-industrial networked economy without including such global urban interdependencies in an urban development policy framework? The next section endeavors to give some answers.

8.3   The Parameters of the Smart City Diplomacy

According to Beaverstock (2002), urban competitiveness, a key objective in various urban development frameworks, including the smart city concept, cannot be fully understood by solely examining internal urban characteristics. Instead, success and competitiveness are shaped by external links and the quality of connections with other global cities. While it is widely accepted that cities don't exist in isolation (Storper, 1997), it's notable that the smart city concept often neglects this global dimension, primarily focusing on internal aspects. This is where smart city diplomacy becomes crucial, serving as an integrating framework in response to globalization, striving to enhance a city's competitiveness (Mursitama and Lee, 2018). This framework essentially incorporates most of the characteristics associated with the smart city concept, as detailed by Tranos and Gertner (2012, pp. 181–185).

First, *digitalization* is a significant megatrend, alongside globalization, demographic change, and climate change, reshaping policies at their core. Over the past two decades, discussions about "smart cities" have been dominated by the integration of digital innovation to create more efficient and livable urban environments (OECD, 2019a). While not exclusive defining factors, new technologies and ICTs play pivotal roles in both world city networks and the smart city concept. At the European level, the URBACT Program has, over the last 15 years, facilitated cities' digital transitions to drive change in urban centers. For example, from 2015 to 2018, Barnsley (UK) led the TechTown URBACT Action Planning Network, exploring how medium-sized cities can generate digital jobs through entrepreneurship, digitalization, or disrupting existing industries. The URBACT methodology and transnational exchange programs helped structure discussions with local and regional tech stakeholders. Globally, the G20 Global Smart Cities Alliance on Technology Governance, established in June 2019, collaborated with experts worldwide to develop a Policy Roadmap for responsible smart cities, validated by 36 "Pioneer Cities" in 2021. Regional city networks were established in Japan, Latin America, and India in the same year to support local implementation, earning the Alliance of the Governance and Economy Award at Smart City Expo World Congress in 2021. The Alliance collaborates with leading international organizations and city networks, receiving founding contributions from C4IR Japan partners, such as Eisai Co., Hitachi, Mori Building, NEC Corporation, NTT Corporation, and Salesforce.com to address governance gaps and advance innovative policy approaches.

Second, as smart city policies aim to *attract businesses* (Hollands, 2008), specific conditions should exist in order to achieve this objective. Cities need to create a vibrant economic environment that can provide the necessary conditions for business growth. Thus, information and communication technologies are not the only components in providing smart solutions. In this context, the capacity of municipalities to involve the various stakeholders (entrepreneurs, academics, non-governmental organizations, and citizens) in planning and implementation processes should be emphasized, as well as their ability to agree on the best solutions for development, responsibilities, and investments as a result of common efforts. At a second level, global links and the position of a city in the world urban hierarchy are also important. Created in 1986, the municipal company "Barcelona Activa", established as a business incubator, was a lead partner of the ACCELMED (Acceleration for Mediterranean Companies) network, which aimed to enhance the growth capacity of Small and Medium-Sized Enterprises (SMEs) in the Mediterranean, in the framework of the Interreg IVB MED. To achieve this, the partners (Milan, Marseille, Bologne, Attika, Ljubljana) developed transnational cooperation tools that facilitated access to finance and support internationalization and business acceleration strategies. Partners developed a crosslanding/softlanding portfolio of services in order to facilitate soft business landing in Mediterranean countries. Furthermore, SME4SMARTCITIES (Mediterranean SME working together to make cities smarter) is an EU-funded project, framed within the ENI CBC Med Program, that intends to strengthen the collaboration between Mediterranean SMEs and cities from Spain (Murcia and Malaga), Italy (Genova), Jordan (Irbid), Israel (Saba), Palestine (Ramallah) around the Smart City sector. The network supported Mediterranean SMEs in order to guarantee that their products and services meet the expectations and needs of smart cities.[1]

Third, a smart city has a *high capacity for innovative activity* and displays elevated levels of entrepreneurship. This objective cannot be achieved without global awareness to attract flows of information, human, and financial capital. Innovative activity is affected, not only by local conditions and regional and urban innovation systems, but also by the position of a city in the dynamic global networks of research and development, business collaboration, finance, and, most importantly, the networks of the creative class usually responsible for the high scores of urban entrepreneurship and innovation. Capacity building, which is an integral component of making smart city strategies a reality, has been actively pursued by subnational networks, such as the United Cities and Local Governments Asia-Pacific (UCLG ASPAC), which promotes cooperation between governments and within wider international communities in the region. Regarding capacity building, UCLG ASPAC specializes in four areas that are of relevance for smart city strategies: sustainable mobility; climate change adaptation and disaster risk reduction; tourism and culture; and local economic development. The essential cooperation between suppliers and city administration is facilitated by an ever-growing number of city networks that try to make solutions interoperable and scalable. In particular, two of them, the World Smart Sustainable Cities Organization (WeGO), based in Seoul, and Open and Agile Smart Cities (OASC), based in Brussels, have developed original instruments to help cities apply the fittest solutions. The first one is mainly present in Asia and Africa and features 158 members, while the second one's 150 members concentrate in Europe and South America (Sala, 2022). WeGO promotes the Smart City Driver, a framework conceived to help cities plan, finance, and deploy smart city projects. The framework includes three interconnected tools (Activator, Solution Finder, Project Implementer). These tools aim to create a junction to exchange the needed basics in setting up smart cities projects. OASC proposes to its members the Minimal Interoperability Mechanism (MIMs), tools based on open technical specifications (a specific level of standardization that covers the technicalities needed to implement products and services), allowing cities to replicate and scale solutions everywhere. MIMs unlock the benefits of interoperability by taking minimal common ground to implement the smart cities standards. Both organizations connect cities and businesses with the world of standards, making them accessible and more immediately applicable to smart cities projects.

Fourth, an inter-urban approach is also necessary for a smart city to achieve goals related to *creativity, innovation and human capital*. All of the three policy objectives found in the core of the smart city conceptualization are linked to a degree with attracting talent at a global level. Cities compete with each other in order to attract such managerial elites, the input of which in the local production system will be valuable. This process places global cities at the top of the spatial division of labor. For instance, the WIT (Welcoming International Talent) city network ran from 2018 until 2021 as URBACT-funded exchange network of seven medium-sized European cities that shared knowledge and experiences about attracting, retaining, and integrating international talents in the city. The participating cities were Groningen (Netherlands-lead partner), Bielsko-Biała (Poland), Debrecen (Hungary), Leuven (Belgium), Magdeburg (Germany), Parma (Italy), and Zlin (Czech Republic).[2]

Lastly, *environmental sustainability* is also an issue that can be approached on a scale larger than that of the local level. Cities, apart from being the main polluters, are highly vulnerable places as they host more than half of Earth's total population. Through global city networks, such as C40, they collaborate to tackle climate change and exchange best practice examples of smart climate solutions that can make cities healthier, greener, and more prosperous. The former mayor of New York, Fiorello La Guardia, famously said "there is no Democratic or Republican way of fixing a sewer". Global city networks, such as the ICLEI, bring together mayors, city officials, and urban planners to share lessons, ideas, and inspiration through peer-to-peer learning. For example, when Paris launched the Velib bike share scheme, just six cities in the C40 network had such systems in place. Today, 43 C40 cities have bike share schemes and Chinese cities are now taking cycle hire to entirely new levels, with hundreds of thousands of bikes transforming travel in Beijing and Shanghai. Similarly, the speed with which Chinese cities have rolled out fleets of electric buses has inspired mayors in European and North American cities to reassess their own targets. In October 2017, 12 cities – London, Paris, Los Angeles, Copenhagen, Barcelona, Quito, Vancouver, Mexico City, Milan, Seattle, Auckland, and

Cape Town – set a goal of procuring only zero emission buses by 2025. Today more than 30 C40 cities have made this commitment by signing the Green and Healthy Streets Declaration. Partnerships drive greater ambition. In 2013, the Chinese County Haiyan that consists of approximately 440,000 citizens, identified best practices in the Danish city Sonderborg. This resulted in a fruitful cooperation between the two cities. By drawing on experiences from the Danish example, Haiyan created (a) a Haiyan ZEROhouse to demonstrate sustainable construction and (b) a sustainable urban development plan for an old part of the city area. In the European framework, Sonderborg is responsible for creating a network through the EU Horizon SmartEnCity project that consists of 28 ambitious European small- and medium-sized cities that aim to be first movers in the smart city transition. The project aims to move European cities toward the Smart Zero Carbon City vision (State of Green, 2019, p. 27). New York City and the City of Copenhagen experienced extreme weather events in 2011 and 2012, respectively. As both coastal cities face rising sea levels and more frequent cloudbursts, they have signed a collaboration agreement that builds upon the successes of their respective resiliency projects. The agreement focuses on climate change adaptation, with an emphasis on cloudburst management. Based on lessons learned from the Climate Resilient Neighbourhood at Østerbro in Copenhagen, the New York Agency Department of Environmental Protection developed a masterplan for a neighborhood in Southeast Queens. The masterplan covers an area with limited storm sewer infrastructure that suffers from flooding. As the Department of Environmental Protection and NYCHA (New York City Housing Agency) use a combination of blue-green and traditional infrastructure, added benefits of CO_2 reductions, increased liveability and biodiversity will ensue (State of Green, 2019, p. 27).

8.4   Conclusions

On 18 March 2019, in the "Athens Road Map on Innovation for Inclusive Growth in Cities" (OECD, 2019b), 60+ Mayors for Inclusive Growth who have made the fight against inequality a priority in their policy agendas called for "leveraging the full potential of technological and digital innovation to build the smart cities of the future and ensure their contribution to better well-being outcomes for all our residents as part of a collaborative, multi-stakeholder process across sectors". On 20 March 2019, in the "Declaration on Policies for Building Better Futures for Regions, Cities and Rural Areas" (OECD, 2019c), Ministers of regional development called, among others, for "connecting all places – regions and cities – to the global economy, by promoting the digitalization of the economy and building regional ecosystems that ink cities and rural areas to support sharing of knowledge, innovation, resources and amenities, and enhance well-being for all residents, leveraging complementarities and valorizing regional diversity and encourage an expanded scope for innovation policy to enhance economic performance, social conditions, and sustainability in all types of regions". One thing is clear: cities, like countries, cannot work alone to build the smart cities of the future. Cities must come together in city diplomacy activities to foster peer-to-peer dialogue for coming up with common solutions to common problems and deliver positive benefits for millions of citizens; helping city leaders and managers better define and build relevant products and services that solve real problems addressing real needs; finding funding opportunities and contract to develop smart city solutions; helping entrepreneurs learn in a few months what they would have learned in years, through mentorship, networking, education, and visibility; and facilitating the collaboration of national, regional, and local governments with innovators and entrepreneurs to match demand and supply, and advise local governments on how to enhance the enabling environment for innovators to deliver.

Notes

1 See https://sme4smartcities.eu/.
2 See https://urbact.eu/networks/welcoming-international-talent.

References

Beaverstock, J.V. (2002) "Transnational Elites in Global Cities: British Expatriates in Singapore's Financial District", *Geoforum*, 33, pp. 525–538.

Bouskela et al. (2016) *The Road towards Smart Cities: Migrating from Traditional City Management to the Smart City*. https://publications.iadb.org/handle/11319/7743#sthash. 4j9oeG Nr. Dpuf.

Caragliu, A., de Bo, C., and Nijkamp, P. (2009) "Smart Cities in Europe", *Proceedings of the 3rd Central European Conference in Regional Science*, Kosice, 7–9 October, pp. 49–59.

Caragliu, A., Del Bo, C., and Nijkamp, P. (2011) "Smart Cities in Europe", *Journal of Urban Technology*, 18 (2), pp. 65–82.

Carrillo, F.J. (2006) *Knowledge Cities*, Oxford: Elsevier.

CEC (2019) *The Future of Cities. Opportunities, Challenges and the Way Forward*, Luxembourg: Publications Office of the European Union.

Centre of Regional Science (2007) *Smart Cities. Ranking of European Medium-Size Cities*, Vienna: Vienna University of Technology.

Dirks, S., Gurdgiev, C., and Keeling, M. (2010) *Smarter Cities for Smarter Growth: How Cities Can Optimize Their Systems for the Talent-Based Economy*, Somers, NY: IBM Global Business Services.

Downey, J., and McGuigan, J. (1999) *Technocities*, London: SAGE.

Dutton, W.H. (1987) *Wired Cities: Shaping the Future of Communications*, London: Macmillan.

Florida, R. (2005) "The World Is Spiky", *Atlantic Monthly*, 296, pp. 48–51.

Giffender, R., Fertner, C., Kramar, H., Kalasek, R., Pichler-Milanović, N., and Meijers, E. (2007) *Smart Cities: Ranking of European Medium-Sized Cities*, Vienna: Centre of Regional Science – Vienna UT.

Hollands, R.G. (2008) "Will the Real Smart City Please Stand Up", *City*, 13 (3), pp. 303–320.

Ishida, T. (2002) "Digital City Kyoto", *Communications of the ACM*, 45 (7), pp. 78–81.

Komninos, N. (2002) *Intelligent Cities*, London: Spon.

Komninos, N. (2006) "The Architecture of Intelligent Cities; Integrating Human, Collective, and Artificial Intelligence to Enhance Knowledge and Innovation", *2nd International Conference on Intelligent Environments*, Athens: Institution of Engineering and Technology.

Komninos, N. (2008) *Intelligent Cities and Globalisation of Innovation Networks*, Abingdon: Routledge.

Komninos, N. (2011) "Intelligent Cities: Variable Geometries of Spatial Intelligence", *Intelligent Buildings International*, 3 (3), pp. 172–188.

Kourtit, K., and Nijkamp, P. (2012) "Smart Cities in the Innovation Age", *Innovation: The European Journal of Social Sciences*, 25 (2), pp. 93–95.

Kourtit, K., Nijkamp, P., and Arribas, D. (2012) "Smart Cities in Perspective – A Comparative European Study by Means of Self-Organizing Maps", *Innovation: The European Journal of Social Sciences*, 25 (2), pp. 229–46.

Lee, J.H., Phaal, R., and Lee, S. (2013) "An Integrated Service-Device-Technology Roadmap for Smart City Development", *Technological Forecasting and Social Change*, 80 (2), pp. 286–306.

Mahizhnan, A. (1999) "Smart Cities: The Singapore Case", *Cities*, 16 (1), pp. 13–18.

Mursitama, T.N., and Lee, L. (2018) "Towards a Framework of Smart City Diplomacy", *Earth and Environmental Science,* 126. https://doi.org/10.1088/1755-1315/126/1/012102.

OECD (2018) *The Policy Implications of Digital Innovation and Megatrends in (smart) Cities of the Future: A Project Proposal*, Paris: OECD.

OECD (2019a) *Enhancing the Contribution of Digitalisation to the Smart Cities of the Future*, Paris: OECD.

OECD (2019b) *Athens Road Map on Innovation for Inclusive Growth in Cities*, OECD, Paris. http://www.oecd-inclusive.com/wp-content/uploads/2019/03/Athens-Roadmap.pdf.

OECD (2019c) *Declaration on Policies for Building Better Futures for Regions, Cities and Rural Areas*, OECD, Paris. http://www.oecd-inclusive.com/wp-content/uploads/2019/03/Athens-Roadmap.pdf

Sala, E. (2022) "Smart City Standards: A Collaboration Challenge?", *City Diplomacy Lab*. https://www.citydiplomacylab.net/category/tools/.

State of Green (2019) "SMART CITIES. Creating Liveable, Sustainable and Prosperous Societies", *State of Green White Papers for a Green Transition*. http://stateofgreen.com/cities.

Storper, M. (1997) "Territories, Flows and Hierarchies in the Global Economy". In K.R. Cox (Ed.) *Spaces of Globalisation*. New York: Guilford.

Thite, M. (2011) "Smart Cities: Implications of Urban Planning for Human Resource Development", *Human Resource Development International*, 14 (5), pp. 623–631.

Thuzar, M. (2011) "Urbanization in SouthEast Asia: Developing Smart Cities for the Future?" In M.S. Montesano and P.O. Lee (Eds.) *Regional Outlook, Southeast Asia 2011-2012*. Singapore: ISEAS Publishing.

Tranos, E., and Gertner, D. (2012) "Smart Networked Cities?", *Innovation: The European Journal of Social Science Research*, 25 (2), pp. 175–190.

UCLG (2012) *SMART CITIES STUDY: International Study on the Situation of ICT, Innovation and Knowledge in Cities*, Bilbao: The Committee of Digital and Knowledge-based Cities of UCLG.

United Nations (2016) UN-Habitat & New Urban Agenda, https://unhabitat.org/the-new-urban-agenda-illustrated

Winters, J.V. (2011) "Why Are Smart Cities Growing? Who Moves and Who Stays", *Journal of Regional Science*, 51 (2), pp. 253–270.

Zygiaris, S. (2013) "Smart City Reference Model: Assisting Planners to Conceptualize the Building of Smart City Innovation Ecosystems", *Journal of the Knowledge Economy*, 4 (2), pp. 217–231.

Part III

The Practice of City Diplomacy

9 The Essentials of City Diplomacy

9.1 Introduction

Although there is a widespread consensus regarding the need of cities engaging in global affairs, city diplomacy practices differ according to a city's particular setting and ability to connect local practices to global impact. First, city's political structure has a significant impact on the stability, longevity, and financial sources of the office of international affairs. The way an office functions in relation to the Mayor's office, boards and committees, and other departments affects its ability and capacity to engage in city diplomacy. Second, capacity refers, not just to the features of different municipal structures, but also to the capabilities and resources available for leading and engaging in municipal diplomacy. Experience in commerce and investment, public diplomacy and international affairs, and strategic communication would be especially helpful. In order to capture and evaluate the impact of city diplomacy initiatives for strategic planning and operational development, it will be critical to close the current skill gap in research and evaluation at local level as city diplomacy becomes an increasingly strategic part of a city's activity. Third, the municipal offices of foreign affairs are usually impacted by a severe lack of resources, as is the case with the majority of newly formed and emerging organizations. Fourth, at a higher level, municipal offices of international affairs also want to establish stronger connections with Ministries, including the Ministries of the Interior, Foreign Affairs, and other government organizations. Fifth, as city diplomacy develops and becomes more prevalent in the community, it is necessary to establish a framework of trust in its interactions with other municipal departments and to more precisely define the role and authority of the organizational setup. Sixth, cities rarely regard their partnerships and collaborative networks as an essential resource, and thus the offices of foreign affairs handle them less strategically, and more on ad hoc basis. Consequently, many cities, though active internationally, do not have a formal, explicit international strategy to encompass the previous parameters of exercising city diplomacy (Karvounis, 2023). However, taking into account the above, an international strategy ensures international engagement of a

DOI: 10.4324/9781003470908-13

municipality, helps in achieving its vision, maximizing the opportunities and benefits for the city. Thus, the aim of this chapter consists of offering practitioners, scholars, and students alike a clear analysis of city diplomacy from the insider's perspective, that is, involving practical reasoning. This chapter will describe the analytical steps needed to put city diplomacy into practice in a more project management frame.

9.2   The Prerequisites of City Diplomacy

The ability of a local authority to create a strategy that satisfies a series of prerequisites is a critical factor in the success of city diplomacy worldwide (Grandi, 2020).

9.2.1   Political Support

City diplomacy requires clear political prioritization for effectiveness and sustainability. The mayor and council must support international partnerships to establish municipal diplomacy as a fully developed public policy. In this respect, the municipality should commit financial and human resources to the international relations office, whereas mayoral responsibilities include representing the city abroad, leading delegations, welcoming foreign dignitaries, promoting the city at international events, advocating for the city's brand, addressing global public opinion, participating in city networks, and attending international summits. Mayors also serve as the main link between state and local diplomacy in democratic, decentralized nations. They play a crucial role in forming cooperative or antagonistic positions on various issues. Some elected leaders may restrict their city's international activity, often in smaller cities, to avoid criticism of wasting taxpayer money without local benefits or due to populist campaigns, emphasizing a "city-first" approach. This is often seen in debates about development aid initiatives and can be linked to insufficient public information on city diplomacy. Such decisions may also reflect a free-rider stance, relying on surrounding cities for international commitments, particularly in policy areas, such as pollution control.

9.2.2   Human Resources

Local governments with a dynamic international strategy typically maintain an international relations office or department staffed by highly qualified individuals. City diplomats share common talents, such as proficiency in foreign languages, negotiation skills, cultural adaptability, and knowledge of international protocol. In certain cases, especially in smaller municipalities, international relations may be handled by the same team responsible for tourism or culture. City diplomats, given the unique nature of their work, have specific responsibilities operating at the intersection of local and international policies. These include gathering and evaluating data on the city's official and informal foreign partnerships, contributing to the strategic plan of city diplomacy, offering advice to the mayor and city council, supporting representatives in meetings abroad, managing bids for international events, overseeing day-to-day communications with foreign partners, developing new partnerships and agreements for international projects, managing the city's relationship with the Ministry of Foreign Affairs, implementing international city branding strategies, overseeing and assessing international projects in various municipal domains, fundraising for international endeavors, managing relations with the local diplomatic community, assisting the press office in covering international affairs, and handling public information and engagement in international activities in the local context.

9.2.3 Economic Resources

There are two main sources of funding for city diplomacy initiatives. First, the self-funded activities are often determined by both local budgets and national legislation. These include the training programs for municipal officers, the locations (monuments, museums, schools, and other public buildings) that the municipality owns or has access to for hosting foreign delegations and international events. Another source of funding is coming from externally sponsored entities, that is, international organizations, development banks, governmental agencies, ministries, embassies, consulates, foreign cultural institutes, non-governmental organizations, and the business sector. This also includes in-kind contributions from public and private partners, such as airlines that offer tickets, hotels that house delegations or museums, and colleges that provide venues and speakers for international events.

9.2.4 Aligning City Diplomacy and State Foreign Policy

Even though subnational governments play a rising role in addressing some of the most urgent global uncertainties, the lack of coordination with central governments hinders the scope of their foreign effort. The absence of a formal discussion channel across the multilayers of European governance diminishes the EU's ability to advance its interest overseas. In this regard, inter-regional connectivity has been at the heart of China's Belt and Road Initiatives, launched in 2013. Both on the Asian and African continents, many cultural and economic partnerships have been tied with local actors. China's town-twinning policy offers a prominent case of regional diplomacy at play. Since the 2000s, the Chinese government has increased by 115% the number of its city partnerships. Although the formal and informal contents of those arrangements vary widely – from education, funding, sports, or culture – they have interestingly raised concerns both in the US and abroad.

9.2.5   *Local Democracy as Integral Part of City Diplomacy*

In recent years, there has been a growing involvement of local public and private stakeholders, including businesses, museums, theaters, artists, schools, colleges, and civil society organizations, in city diplomacy efforts. They play a crucial role in the planning and execution of city diplomacy initiatives (see town-twinning committees). Whatever shape the cooperation takes, it usually enables the municipality to gain from the imagination, vigor, and political backing of local actors as well as their established international ties. In return, local performers get the chance to fulfill their own ambitions and get exposure and experience abroad. These collaborations therefore serve as the main means of responding to the critique that has been raised, which characterizes city diplomacy as a strategy lacking in "return on investment" and a palpable influence on the region. Furthermore, they serve as the impetus behind global initiatives that align with the demands of local communities and interested parties. Municipalities all over the world have created a range of communication and engagement tools, including seminars, social media, press releases, and conferences, to create the ideal environment for the growth of local partnerships.

9.3   The Practicalities of City Diplomacy

It is vital that every local authority participating in an international partnership takes into account certain practical parameters of this relationship (Handley, 2006, pp. 19–21), so as not to expose itself in the course of implementation of specific initiatives, as well as the state and the national authorities it represents abroad.

9.3.1   *Code of Conduct*

The management of public money, on the one hand, and the projection of the image of the country abroad, on the other, require that all elected municipal officials and the local authority employees are subject to individual codes of conduct, either whenever the individuals are undertaking official duties, or during their contacts made within the framework of the town-twinning relationships.

9.3.2   *Transparency in Economic Transactions*

Local authorities should ensure that there is a procedure in place to demonstrate that careful consideration has been given to every financial transaction, particularly in the case of expenditure relating to travel and accommodation. For officer and member participation, there should be a process to explain the reasons for the visit/meeting and the pursued benefits.

9.3.3 Re-energizing a Partnership

In several cases, a local authority enters into partnerships that have no further continuity because the people responsible for setting up the link may no longer be there or able to drive the link and create new interest. The practice of some local authorities suggests several ways of revitalizing an interest for a town-twinning or international partnership that has remained inactive for many years (e.g., joint proposal in the framework of an EU program, cultural exchanges).

9.3.4 Re-educating the Locals

For many people the concept of city diplomacy, for instance, is either completely unknown or misunderstood. To increase, therefore, interest, it is necessary to explain exactly what city diplomacy is about. Actively promoting its dynamic and wide-ranging aspects and tools will help, through events, exhibitions, and workshops that may be seen by schools, associations, and representatives of economic and social agencies.

9.3.5 Activities of High Relevance

Activities need to be relevant. The various forms of city diplomacy are set up on the basis of friendship and culture and, while these values should underpin all links, times have moved on and city diplomacy forms, like all other aspects of society, must reflect current trends and priorities.

9.3.6 Giving People a Voice

The planning of the events should be the outcome of direct consultations between local authorities and members of the community, making thus activities more appealing to local people.

9.3.7 Youth Initiatives

The involvement of young people in activities and programs that interest them, such as the construction of websites, the dissemination of leaflets for hosting an international event, the organizing of athletic and musical events, etc., can make a difference to how people feel about a city diplomacy link.

9.3.8 Targeting New Members

Usually several members within a local community appear to be reluctant to display any interest for city diplomacy initiatives, so that the relevant communication campaigns, through social media, must reach their work or leisure places (i.e. leisure centers, libraries, community halls).

9.3.9   New Partnerships at Home

As part of the re-energizing process, organizers can use the opportunity to look for new partners or sponsors within the local community, such as large businesses or academic institutions. This is an ideal opportunity to make new alliances at home.

9.3.10   Window of Opportunity for Internal Re-organization and Commitment

A city diplomacy initiative appears as a challenge for an internal re-organization and re-structuring of a local authority. City diplomacy activities require the full engagement and commitment of a municipality's personnel, not just the staff of the competent department or office. Training sessions for city diplomacy activities cannot be limited to the project managers of particular international partnerships. The whole organizations should exhibit the required commitment and devotion to the goals of the international strategy, making thus easier the adoption of good practices and the devotion to the necessary internal restructuring of municipal units for the implementation of this strategy.

9.4   The Design of a City Diplomacy Strategy

There are no agreed typologies for classifying the international relations of local governments; nor are there any set rules for initiating, or carrying through, the transnational strategies of cities. Far from that, these will vary according to the local context, motivations, and specific goals of each local authority. Practice has demonstrated that each municipality has a broad margin of maneuver and creativity to innovate when it comes to forging international bonds. While we do not intend to give step-by-step directions, below are some general guidelines that may prove useful for planning an international strategy (CEC, 2005; Institute of International Sociology, 2015).

9.4.1   Assessing the External Context

An internationalization strategy cannot be based only on a local government's needs. The possibilities available must also be taken into consideration. To find out its international potential, a local authority must identify the threats, as well as the opportunities that are beyond its direct control. This assessment calls for a thorough analysis of the background and current situation of the city's international relations. The process entails identifying international links in every area of local life and drawing up an inventory of those key players with bonds beyond national borders (universities, companies, immigrants' communities, cultural, artistic and sports associations, chambers of commerce, etc.). It is also important to consider other tiers, such as neighboring city councils, provincial or regional governments and the central state, and to become familiar with foreign policy principles and priorities, as well as with the current status of diplomatic relations. To that end, information must be obtained on the existing bilateral and multilateral cooperation programs. The analysis of the external context must further include an evaluation of the current political, economic, and social situation in the country, the region, and the global scene. Furthermore, there should be a comprehensive evaluation of the legal framework for the city's international action, taking into consideration both national and international law.

9.4.2 Analyzing the Internal Situation

After analyzing the external context, it's crucial to research the internal situation of the local government and the territory, identifying strengths and weaknesses. Ask questions, such as: What motivates the local authority to establish international relations? What results does it expect? Is the institution ready for international cooperation, and what resources are available? Understand the legal framework and the city council's maneuvering space in international affairs. Study different authority areas and departments to identify existing or potential international links. Administrative aspects and internal policy mechanisms, including day-to-day decision-making practices, are vital. This analysis should not only follow formal rules, but also describe the actual decision-making process objectively. Consider staff qualifications, administrative procedures, and the work environment. Lastly, assess the territory's strengths and weaknesses, including its history, location, production, social and cultural characteristics, and natural features, to set the stage for the local government' international positioning.

9.4.3 Identifying Local Priorities

Local governments, as part of their planning, should incorporate international relations into their Local Development, Operational, or Strategic Plan, clearly defining policies and priorities. After analyzing both internal and external contexts, it's essential to identify priorities aligned with the goals outlined in the plan. This ensures that international actions contribute to achieving the local authority's objectives. By integrating international relations into the strategic agenda, cities can leverage their potential across various sectors. Priority identification is a crucial step, forming the basis for setting specific goals and planning relevant activities in any strategy. Local authorities may use various criteria, such as thematic, historical, cultural, geographic, or linguistic, to identify transnational priorities. The challenge is to align international priorities with local ones, often leading local governments to collaborate with partners who share similar concerns. Establishing links with similar partners facilitates the exchange of experiences in areas, such as urban planning, public transport, environmental pollution, and social policies.

9.4.4   Defining a Vision for the Future

After analyzing the external and internal contexts and defining local priorities, the local government can articulate a future vision for its international strategy aligned with the general mission and Local Development Plan. This vision should guide the organization's actions beyond national borders for the next 5, 10, or 20 years. The envisioned future for the city on the global stage includes:

- Having global projection and visibility akin to a prestigious city "brand".
- Being identified by a specific feature, public policy, or international event.
- Being recognized by national authorities and other local governments as a player with links beyond national borders.
- Participating in major national, regional, and international municipal forums and associations.
- Serving as a global stakeholder with its own political and economic standing and identity.
- Engaging in international campaigns and efforts to improve living conditions and protect the global environment.
- Having partners beyond national borders for specific goals (town-twinning, friend cities, international bodies, foundations, international NGOs, etc.).
- Playing an active role in decentralized cooperation through capacity building and direct local government experience sharing.
- Receiving and offering technical assistance in priority areas of the local agenda.
- Attracting international investments, tourism, and trade for local economic development.
- Participating in international programs and projects to enhance the quality of life and public services.
- Implementing an international solidarity policy, aiding other city councils abroad in emergencies or natural disasters.
- Boosting international relations for local stakeholders and the population through civic education activities.
- Adopting a foreign policy stance in international conflicts, favoring peace, tolerance, cooperation, and opposing discrimination of any kind.

9.4.5   Implementing the Strategy

The implementation of the international strategy involves defining actions and developing activities. After identifying the international priorities of the local government, the next step is to establish both general and specific objectives. Objectives, as goals, guide actions to achieve desired results. In the context of a strategic plan, objectives go beyond day-to-day operations, focusing on vital endeavors in the medium and long term. Additionally, the local authority should develop procedures for internal communication to raise

Table 9.1 The Master Plan of the Canary Islands Government-Spain

---

General objective

To promote sustainable human, social and economic development in order to eradicate poverty in the world.

Specific objectives

a To foster the development of the more disadvantaged nations by providing them with economic and material resources, so as to help them achieve economic and social growth on a more equitable basis.

b To favor such nations' self-sustained development based on the beneficiaries' own capacities, promoting a better standard of living for the population – particularly the poorest sectors – as well as due respect for fundamental human rights.

c To work toward more balanced political, strategic, economic and commercial relations, thereby promoting a stable, safe scenario for international peace.

d To prevent and assist in emergency situations by carrying out humanitarian aid actions.

e To favor the organization and consolidation of democratic systems of government, as well as respect for fundamental human rights.

f To foster political, economic and cultural relations with developing nations in accordance with the principles and objectives of cooperation.

Source: Garesché (2007).

awareness and promote the implementation of the international strategy. The international dimension should be a regular item on the agenda for all partnerships. Representatives should also highlight the international dimension in sub-regional, regional, and national networks as appropriate. Within the municipal council, the international dimension should be a regular item on every meeting agenda. Municipal networks can leverage sub-regional, regional, national, and international networks to maximize benefits and assist in achieving objectives (Table 9.1).

9.4.6 Monitoring and Controlling the International Strategy

After the actions are defined, their impacts and results must be taken into consideration. These are the consequences of the actions and the link between actions and specific objectives. For instance, for an initiative titled "creating a new festival that will travel between the partner municipalities", the impact can be "creation of new opportunity for tourism". This in turn leads to the fulfillment of the specific objective "developing the tourism sector in the area", which helps with the general objective "improving the economy of the area". Once the impacts are decided, indicators to monitor them must be chosen. The indicators should be objectively verifiable and should be quantitative measures of the results of the actions. For example, regarding the impact "creation of new opportunity for tourism", an indicator could be "number of tourists that visited the area". Once the indicators are decided, a monitoring and evaluation framework for their analysis must be put in place. This framework depends upon the indicators chosen and can include official statistics or external analysis as sources of data. Regarding the indicator "number of tourists that visited the area", a possible source of data can be the statistical offices (e.g., number of tickets issued/sold) of the involved municipalities.

Ideally, the definition of such a strategy should be renewed at any municipal election, to integrate it into the administration's operational program.

9.5   Conclusions

As seen throughout this chapter, a local government takes different paths to undertake an international strategy or establish long-lasting international cooperation relations. This chapter has suggested that these are not "one-way" roads, nor do they necessarily entail a strict logical order or chronological sequence. The recommendations set out in this chapter are intended to help local governments build their strategies and advance at their own pace, according to the priorities imposed by their specific realities. Practice shows that internationalization strategy is progressive and that the vision is continuously fed back by practice, experience, and the passing of time. In short, the success of the local governments' internationalization process, regardless of their specific situation, depends on its ability to be proactive, that is, take the initiative and open up to the world; be receptive, that is, bring the world to its city; be realistic and focused on what can actually reasonably be achieved; strengthen technical capabilities and skills; coordinate and communicate within the local government; limit red tape; establish targets and impact; and anticipate changes and innovate.

References

CEC (2005) *Aid Delivery Methods – Project Cycle Management Guidelines*, European Commission: Publications Office.

Garesché, E.D.Z. (2007) *Guidelines for the International Relations of Local Governments and Decentralised Cooperation between the European Union and Latin America*, Vol. 1, Practical Manual for the Internationalisation of Cities, Diputación de Barcelona.

Grandi, L.K. (2020) *City Diplomacy*, Cham: Palgrave Macmillan.

Handley, S. (2006) *Take Your Partners. The Local Authority Handbook on International Partnerships*, London: Local Government International Bureau.

Institute of International Sociology (2015) *City to City Cooperation Toolkit*, Gorizia: Council of Europe.

Karvounis, A. (2023) *City Diplomacy and the Europeanisation of Local Government. The Prospects of Networking in the Greek Municipalities*, Cham: Palgrave Macmillan.

10 The Impact of City Diplomacy

10.1 Introduction

Despite the growing awareness of the usefulness of a unique voice for local authorities on global problems through their networking initiatives, determining the precise impact of those international bilateral or multilateral partnerships has been truly challenging. Today, it is not enough to organize or attend an international event whose only results are the minutes and a list of participants. "Impact" should be gauged, for instance, by the changes brought about, at least, in the life of the city-dwellers and by its transformation potential in the medium and long term. True, the international partnerships of local authorities appear to have the potential to have an impact on local policy due to their proliferation among municipalities. But not all the types of city diplomacy have equal impact. In a recent research (Pejic et al., 2022), respondents were asked which types of international engagement have had the greatest impact on their city's policymaking. City networking was overwhelmingly the most common response, selected by 81% of cities. In such a context, the role of municipal staff in charge of international relations becomes all the more crucial. Their search for the best network should be based on assessing the impact of networks on the areas identified as political priorities by the cities. This impact though has been identified to take on different shapes depending on the intermediate factors at national level. Most of the literature thus limits its focus to the interaction between city networks and members and ignores the impacts of the other forms of city diplomacy (Busch et al., 2018, p. 224). In this respect, this chapter will explore the theoretical approaches and the various narratives of city diplomacy's impact, along with the intermediate variables.

10.2 The Theoretical Framework of the City Diplomacy Impact

"Impact" means changes in policies, politics, and polities at the international, national, and local levels as a result of the participation of local authorities in various forms of city diplomacy. As a result, most of the scholarly

DOI: 10.4324/9781003470908-14

contributions approach critically the local and national contexts that regulate the impact of the activities of local authorities at the international level.

In particular, the issue of actual efficiency has been partially approached by the literature (Provan and Kenis, 2007; Turrini et al., 2010), but at a very general level. As Ward and Williams (1997, p. 441) have argued, these approaches do not contribute to the understanding of the international partnerships as long as, it is suggested, there appears to be a lack of work on the tangible impact of city networking (Acuto and Rayner, 2016, p. 1149). On the other hand, reports produced by city networks underline the enthusiasm shown by cities over the last few decades, as they believe that city networking offers substantial benefits. A recent series of reports by C40 cities and ARUP on Climate Action in Megacities, the Powers for Climate Action, and the Potential for Climate Action (a series of studies created in collaboration with the UCL City Leadership Lab) all emphasized the influence of city diplomacy and, in particular, of C40 cities network, in providing preliminary evidence that cooperative modes of urban governance are bringing about transformative action in cities (Acuto et al., 2017, p. 17). Likewise, Krause (2012) measured the impact of the International Council for Local Environmental Initiatives (ICLEI) in the US by reviewing the activities undertaken by member cities (more than 600). The results varied from an increase of 3–to 36% in activities compared to non-networked cities. This outcome could be explained by the role that the ICLEI plays as a provider of technical advice, as a forum of exchange and as a supervisor of progress (Krause, 2012). Similar results were found in two megacities in Brazil, where the role of the ICLEI has been central to mitigating GHG emissions (D'Almeida Martins and da Costa Ferreira, 2011). In both cases, city networks have more impact where national governments are not committed.

In the realm of international partnerships among local authorities, the shift from individual learning of local officers to organizational change or enhanced administrative capabilities poses an open question. Johnson and Thomas (2007) found that individual learning can foster organizational capability when the individual wields sufficient influence as a change agent. However, this alone is insufficient. Factors, such as the individual's learning style, education quality, organizational elements, and internal resistance within units, are crucial in the challenging process of organizational change. The exchange of best practices and human resource training is proposed as a multi-level learning process that involves transferring policies, structures, and institutions among territorial authorities, shaping new terms for local governance (Dolowitz and Marsh, 1996, p. 344). Carla Tedesco (2010), analyzing Bari and Venice's participation in URBACT project-bound city networks, found that the transfer of innovative practices affects member cities differently. Venice, leading a network on social inclusion, actively participated, while Bari only gained information about innovative projects (Tedesco, 2010, p. 193). Chorianopoulos (2003) supports this impact variety, noting that

European project-bound city networks often reflect governance culture from northern countries, making it challenging for southern countries to fully adopt and implement policies due to fund absorption concerns. Malé (2019, p. 36) suggests that thematic city network platforms serve as effective interchange mechanisms, but fall short of driving structural transformation.

In assessing the environmental impact of international city networks, Bouteligier notes that these networks tend to excel in organizing international activities structurally, but often fall short of producing clear changes in behavior or improving environmental conditions (Bouteligier, 2011, p. 234). Tangible results, when achieved, typically stem from long-term collaborations involving permanent employees of partner cities (Keiner and Kim, 2007; Kern and Bulkeley, 2009, p. 316). The engagement of local authorities' employees or competent departments linking network initiatives with the municipality is crucial in determining the network's impact at the local level. As a result, many cities fail to see their participation in international partnerships as part of a larger internationalization strategy (Abdullah and Garcia-Chueca, 2020, p. 4), as seen in the previous chapter.

Bearing in mind the above contributions, here we propose that the impact of the international partnerships of local authorities can be classified into various forms: cognitive, funding, administrative, political and sustainable.

10.3   The Types of City Diplomacy Impact

In this sense, this book briefly introduces five types of city diplomacy impact that function, more often, as overlapping processes: cognitive, administrative, funding, political, and sustainable.

10.3.1   The Cognitive Impact

The current literature on international partnerships often focuses on the transfer of various types of knowledge and policy learning (Johnson and Thomas, 2007; King, 2002; Van Ewijk and Baud, 2009; Wilson and Johnson, 2007). In recent years, there has been a shift in many cities' preference for international ties from perpetual bilateral projects to shorter-term international projects, involving two or more foreign partners. This approach is driven by city leaders' desire to leverage the potential of city diplomacy to positively impact the city. Many of these international projects involve the exchange of best practices in various municipal sectors, such as transportation, hygiene, and the introduction of new technologies. This trend is often associated with the proliferation of regional integration. Regional organizations, such as the European Union, the Council of Europe, ASEAN, the African Union, and Mercosur view cities as key actors in strengthening ties between their member countries. Consequently, these organizations have created funding frameworks or supported existing ones to enhance cooperation through calls for projects, knowledge exchange, and events. This dynamic has also contributed to the expansion of triangular (or North-South-South) cooperation, connecting a city from the Global North with two cities from the Global South (Grandi, 2020, p. 16). Radaelli (2000) characterizes the European Union as a "platform for the mass transfer of know-how". In particular, the project-bound EU networks, within the framework of cooperation programs, such as INTERREG and URBACT, promote exchange and learning on sustainable urban development among cities as well as the inclusion of capacity-building measures and pilots on implementation and transfer. For instance, the Department of International Cooperation along with the Organisation of Culture, Sports and Youth of the municipality of Athens showed a particular interest in Eurocities, which was considered as an additional resource for the municipality, through the exchange of good practices over the social integration of the immigrants, as well as in the way of organizing social services based on the expertise and valuable experience gained from the municipal authority's active participation in the network's workshops (Municipality of Athens, 2015, pp. 14, 33).

10.3.2   The Administrative Impact

Administrative impact refers to the capitalization of the above exchange of experiences, innovative approaches, and capacity building and their subsequent translation into changes in the way policymakers at the local level address needs and challenges. The truth is that international networking is seen by cities as a possibility to escape the narrow confines of national policymaking, as a political source for legitimizing efforts to modernize local political-administrative systems and to break up with traditional political cultures and belief systems (Hamedinger, 2011, p. 94). Van Ewijk and Baud (2009) have raised the issue of the practical application of transferred practices and policies. More specifically, they underline, adopting the position of Argyris (1999), that learning takes place only when knowledge is applied at a practical level, giving, for example, a solution to a daily problem. For instance, the city of Örebo (SE) developed a "sustainable urban transport plan" as part of a project-bound European city network, including 11 local authorities from the countries around the Baltic Sea (2005–2007) (Montin, 2011, p. 85). Of course, even in cases where the production and transfer of innovative knowledge at the international level is achieved, this does not mean that this is translated into practical application (Stone, 2004).

10.3.3   The Funding Impact

A significant part of the literature on city diplomacy and networking is criticized because it focuses mainly on local authorities' main motivation factor, that is, seeking to secure resources from funding programs through networking (Huggins, 2013, p. 5). More specifically, it is argued that cities can exploit economies of scale in modern forms of collaboration (Capello, 2000). The city networking, as a potential means of accessing international and European funding, provides an opportunity for them to plan their projects without the intermediation of the national authority. For many cities, funding is more than financing transformation projects; the attached rules, regulations, and instruments prescribe ways of understanding problems, forms of behavior and action and can be included in their "ordinary" management activities (Atkinson and Rossignolo, 2010, p. 204). Behind, although, active participation within international partnerships, there are also narrow self-interests. A motive can be to obtain extra resources for a development project that would begin anyway. For instance, professional officials in Swedish municipalities might not regard themselves as having anything to learn from other less-professionalized municipal organizations in Europe and participate in project-bound city networks simply because there is some potential additional funding (Montin, 2011, p. 88).

10.3.4   The Political Impact

The potential political impact of city diplomacy involves positioning cities more boldly on the global stage. Faced with pressing global challenges, many mayors worldwide choose to position their cities as hubs of innovation and active engagement. Consequently, cities have gained recognition as global actors across various policy sectors, including migration, global health, climate change, sustainability, human rights, social justice, development cooperation, and counterterrorism (Busch, 2015; Creutz, 2023). Key international organizations, such as UN-Habitat, the World Health Organization (WHO), and UNESCO, have played pivotal roles in advancing city networking with the establishment of institutional features and dedicated secretariats. The growing interaction between international organizations and cities is evident in initiatives, such as the appointment of a UN Special Envoy on Cities and Climate Change. Notable examples of cities' involvement include the drafting of the Global Compact on Migration in 2019 and the World Bank entering legal agreements on urban development projects directly with cities. This pragmatic relationship acknowledges cities as direct contributors to policymaking, decision-making, and policy implementation, recognizing them as targets of international organizations' policies. A 2020 study on city diplomacy revealed a prevailing belief among city leaders that cities have a more substantial impact on global challenges compared to national governments (Kosovac et al., 2020). In particular, on the issue of EU social policy, cities become means of influence, mainly through their participation in Eurocities and the relatively recent Network of Local Authority Observatories, to promote their policies at national and European levels (Asdourian and Ingenhoff, 2020, p. 86). In 2013, the municipality of Kos joined the European Network of Cities and Regions for the Social Economy (REVES). According to the municipal officers, "a channel of communication is being opened with the European decision-making centres …", in order to "develop a direct cooperation with major European bodies of the social economy".[1]

10.3.5   The Sustainable Impact

Sustainable impact is synonymous with changes in urban governance in five discrete ways. First, member cities of an international partnership have the responsibility to contribute to the production of a strategic plan (see Chapter 9) for all their international engagements or capacity-building plans and consequently cultivate a proper organizational environment favorably receptive to change and innovation. In this respect, the municipalities that organizationally create the conditions for successful participation in international partnerships and instill the international "networking culture" across the entire local administration contribute to some form of sustainable impact. The creation of the appropriate environment for the exploitation and internalization of the "changes" entailed by participation in an international partnership is a potential guarantee for a continuous trajectory of adoption and implementation of innovative practices. Organizational factors and resistance from within the organizational departments play a decisive role ("uncomfortable process of organizational change") in this procedure (Johnson and Thomas, 2007). For instance, the municipality of Amaroussion (GR) was the only municipality in Greece in 2004 that introduced and implemented a quality system based on the ISO 9001:2000 quality system, the environmental management system (EMAS) and the Common Assessment Framework (CAF), before it set up the European network titled "Q-cities" (Cities with Quality) in 2007.[2] Second, the long-term approach to international partnerships is another aspect of the sustainable impact. In the framework of a strategy plan, international networking goes beyond merely quantitative terms of the number of partnerships a local authority takes part in, or even the passive attitude of rule-takers in various ad hoc, temporary or permanent networks. In this sense, the partner cities are seen as an extra resource for officers or elected representatives in the daily management of local affairs. Therefore, the related partnership is not seen as a one-off public relations exercise but as an important component in the life cycle of policymaking at the local level. Third, the member cities of a partnership may exploit their dynamics beyond the time-frame and the specific deliverables of a particular project, as well as the relevant facilitating knowledge or practice sharing activities, and subsequently engender the conditions for setting up a long-term collaboration, either with the same or other partners within the particular or other policy domain of this relationship. For instance, the municipality of Neapolis-Sykies (GR) took part in the project-bound *SOLIDA* network of municipalities from Croatia, Slovenia, Portugal, Spain, Italy, Malta, and Greece which led to a more permanent structure of collaboration, that is, the establishment of the traditional city network titled *SOLIDA*-Network of Solidarity Based-Towns.[3] Fourth, the sustainability of the results of well-built partnerships is ensured when the corresponding local communities are coherently woven into the member cities' international strategies. In this respect, city diplomacy expresses the willingness of citizens to have another point of access to international affairs, and thus, local democracy can become the barometer of the sustainable impact. In particular, project-bound EU (URBACT) networks are based around the collaboration between city authorities and local stakeholders in local support groups. Ninety-seven percent of URBACT III networked cities, having completed this process considered that the participatory approach used during their network, would continue afterward (Karvounis, 2023, p. 282). Fifth, lastly, sustainable impact rests on the coordination of a local authority with national government, being in permanent contact with the official diplomacy and complementing national agenda. Furthermore, sustainability also depends on the collaboration with other levels of government, which secures that there is no institutional competition and overlapping (Van der Pluijm and Melissen, 2007, p. 13).

10.4 The Intermediate Factors of City Diplomacy Impact

As highlighted in the literature, the intervening variables that influence the achievement of reform alignment within a country vary across systems and actors. So, despite the reforming zeal of several municipalities, the internal conditions, the so-called "intermediate factors" (Heritier and Knill, 2001), such as economic hardship, lack of appropriate support structure and communication between organizational units and the absence of culture of intermunicipal cooperation, resistance to the "new", political choices, and adjustment difficulties, moderate the modernization dynamic and the impact process. Bouteligier (2013, pp. 94–95), examining the internal and external dimensions of international multilateral partnerships for the environment, argues that there is a distance, a gap between the exchange of good practices and their application. Bouteligier notes that the national context and the institutional and structural differences between partner cities stand as obstacles to the implementation of these practices. So, studying the Metropolis and C40 networks, Bouteligier concluded that "there is a gap between sharing knowledge about best practices – which happens to be very successful – and implementing best practices elsewhere, which is very difficult to achieve" (Bouteligier, 2013, p. 94). In this respect, Bomberg and Peterson (2000) remain cautious about the impact of European networking activity, since they consider that the influence of local government at the European level is determined by the national constitutional framework, mentioning the German Länder as having infinitely more influence at the European level, in comparison to UK local authorities, as they enjoy greater autonomy (Bomberg and Peterson, 2000, p. 234). Finally, the complex procedures and requirements for resources, in the context of territorial cooperation programs, as well as the excessive expectations for the outcome of these partnerships, are considered an insurmountable obstacle for the diffusion of reform practices among the member cities of the networks (Dühr and Nadin, 2007; Waterhout and Stead, 2007).

In a study of the European city networking of 162 Greek municipalities during the 2007–2013 and 2014–2020 programming periods, Karvounis (2023) argued that reform and counter-reform are at the heart of a considerable number of the international cooperative actions of municipalities. The main intermediate factors identified were related to political choices, the inability of the involved organizational units of the municipalities to express a technocratic discourse, the organizational deficits at the level of structures and personnel, the limitations of the bureaucracy, and, in general, a cultural context that did not tolerate changes. For instance, although the "international specialisation of the city of Heraklion" was sought through multilateral collaborations, problems of "insufficient staffing of the European programs office" were pointed out, while the "lack of culture in matters of intermunicipal cooperation" also hindered the international strategic goals of the local authority (Municipality of Heraklion, 2013, p. 448). Likewise, Thessaloniki decided about the non-necessity of the existence of a support structure for the participation of the municipality (since 2013) in the European Alliance of Cities against Racism (ECCAR). Moreover, in some major municipalities, there has been a fragmentation and diffusion of responsibility and competence for monitoring their membership of city networks. For instance, in 2014, the monitoring of Athens' membership of European city networks had been assigned to six municipal organizational units and legal entities, with apparent gaps of coordination.

10.5   Conclusions

The various forms of city diplomacy impact are basically overlapping, sometimes contradictory, but certainly multifaceted. We cannot come up with a secure answer *a priori* about the form of impact that may result from an international engagement of a local authority. The needs, the motives, the operational program (if any), the socio-economic characteristics, and the internal and external environments ("intermediate factors") of the involved municipalities determine the impact of their international engagements. One cannot expect that municipalities engaged with the same international partnership would exhibit the same impact. In other words, the common challenges do not necessarily lead to similar institutional changes both at the level of the content and at the rate of development of the changes. The same stimulus often produces different local results.

Notes

1 Interview with Ms. A. Georgoudakis, executive officer of the Directorate of Planning, Organisation and Informatics of the municipality of Kos (13 July 2014).
2 Interview with Mr. M. Christakis, General Secretary of the municipality of Amaroussion (6 May 2014).
3 Interview with Mr. G. Polichroniadis, Head of the Independent Department of Programming, Development, E-Government and IT of the municipality of Neapoli-Sykies (2 September 2022).

References

Abdullah, H., and Garcia-Chueca, E. (2020) "Cacophony or Complementarity? The Expanding Ecosystem of City Networks Under Scrutiny". In S. Amiri and E. Sevin (Eds.) *City Diplomacy. Current Trends and Future Prospects* (pp. 37–58). Basingstoke: Palgrave Macmillan.

Acuto, M., Morissette, M., and Tsouros, A. (2017) "City Diplomacy: Towards More Strategic Networking? Learning with WHO Healthy Cities", *Global Policy*, 8 (1), pp. 14–21.

Acuto, M., and Rayner, S. (2016) "City Networks: Breaking Gridlocks or Forging (New) Lock-ins?", *International Affairs*, 92 (5), pp. 1147–1166.

Argyris, C. (1999) *On Organisational Learning*, Oxford: Blackwell.

Asdourian, B., and Ingenhoff, D. (2020) "A Framework of City Diplomacy on Positive Outcomes and Negative Emotional Engagement: How to Enhance the International Role of Cities and City/Mayor Branding on Twitter?". In S. Amiri and E. Sevin (Eds.) *City Diplomacy. Current Trends and Future Prospects* (pp. 83–109). Basingstoke: Palgrave Macmillan.

Atkinson, R., and Rossignolo, C. (2010) "Cities and the 'soft side' of Europeanisation: The Role of Urban Networks". In A. Hamedinger and A. Wolffhardt (Eds.) *The Europeanisation of Cities, Urban Change and Urban Networks* (pp. 197–225). Amsterdam: Techne Press.

Bomberg, E., and Peterson, J. (2000) "Policy Transfer and Europeanisation: Passing the Heineken Test?", *Queen's Papers on Europeanisation*, No. 2, Belfast: Institute of European Studies, Queen's University of Belfast.

Bouteligier, S. (2011) "Global Cities and Networks for Global Environmental Governance", *Ph.D.*, Leuven: KU Leuven.

Bouteligier, S. (2013) *Cities, Networks, and Global Environmental Governance. Spaces of Innovation, Places of Leadership*, New York and London: Routledge.

Busch, H. (2015) "Linked for Action? An Analysis of Transnational Municipal Climate Networks in Germany", *International Journal of Urban Sustainable Development*, 7 (2), pp. 213–231.

Busch, H., Bendlin, L., and Fenton, P. (2018) "Shaping Local Response – The Influence of Transnational Municipal Climate Networks on Urban Climate Governance", *Urban Climate*, 24, pp. 221–230.

Capello, R. (2000) "The City-Network Paradigm: Measuring Urban Network Externalities", *Urban Studies*, 37 (11), pp. 1925–1945.

Chorianopoulos, I. (2003) "North–South Local Authority and Governance Differences in EU Networks", *European Planning Studies*, 11 (6), pp. 671–695.

Creutz, K. (2023) "Cities as Global Actors. Bringing Governance Closer to the People", *Briefing Paper*, 354, February, Finnish Institute of International Affairs.

D'Almeida Martins, R., and da Costa Ferreira, L. (2011) "Opportunities and Constraints for Local and Subnational Climate Change Policy in Urban Areas: Insights from Diverse Contexts", *International Journal of Global Environmental Issues*, 11 (1), pp. 37–53.

Dolowitz, D., and Marsh, D. (1996) "Who Learns What from Whom: A Review of the Policy Transfer Literature", *Political Studies*, 44 (2), pp. 343–357.

Dühr, S., and Nadin, V. (2007) "Europeanisation through Transnational Territorial Cooperation? The Case of INTERREG IIIB North-West Europe", *Planning Practice and Research*, 22 (3), pp. 373–394.

Grandi, L.K. (2020) *City Diplomacy*, Cham: Palgrave Macmillan.

Hamedinger, A. (2011) "Resisitng Europeanisation? Continuities and Change in Governance in Vienna". In E.V. Bever, H. Reynaert and K. Steyvers (Eds.) *The Road to Europe: Main Street or Backwards Alley for Local Governments in Europe?* (pp. 93–115). Brugge: Vanden Broele Publishers.

Heritier, A., and Knill, C. (2001) "Differential Responses to European Policies: A Comparison". In A. Heritier, D. Kerwer, C. Knill, A.-C. Douillet, D. Lehmkuhl and M. Teutsch (Eds.) *Differential Europe. The European Union Impact on National Policymaking* (pp. 257–294). Lanham, MD: Rowman and Littlefield.

Huggins, C. (2013) "Motivations behind Local Government Transnational Networking", *Regional Insights*, 4 (1), pp. 9–11.

Johnson, H., and Thomas, A. (2007) "Individual Learning and Building Organisational Capacity for Development", *Public Administration and Development*, 26 (1), pp. 39–48.

Karvounis, A. (2023) *City Diplomacy and the Europeanisation of Local Government. The Prospects of Networking in the Greek Municipalities*, Cham: Palgrave.

Keiner, M., and Kim, A. (2007) "Transnational City Networks for Sustainability", *European Planning Studies*, 15 (10), pp. 1369–1395.

Kern, K., and Bulkeley, H. (2009) "Cities, Europeanisation and Multi-Level Governance: Governing Climate Change through Transnational Municipal Networks", *Journal of Common Market Studies*, 47 (2), pp. 309–332.

King, K. (2002) "Banking on Knowledge: The New Knowledge Projects of the World Bank", *Compare*, 32 (3), pp. 311–326.

Kosovac, A., Hartley, K., Acuto, M., and Gunning, D. (2020) *Conducting City Diplomacy. A Survey of International Engagement in 47 Cities*, Chicago-Parkville: The Chicago Council on Global Affairs & Connected Cities Lab.

Krause, R.M. (2012) "An Assessment of the Impact that Participation in Local Climate Networks Has on Cities' Implementation of Climate, Energy, and Transportation Policies", *Review of Policy Research*, 29 (5), pp. 585–604.

Malé, J.-P. (2019) "The Emergence of City Alliances and Fronts: Towards New Forms of Local Government Influence?". In A. Fernández de Losada and H. Abdullah (Eds.) *Rethinking the Ecosystem of International City Networks* (pp. 31–37). Barcelona: Cidob Edicions.

Montin, S. (2011) "Swedish Local Government in Multilevel Governance". In E. Van Bever, H. Reynaert and K. Steyvers (Eds.) *The Road to Europe – Main Street or Backwards Alley for Local Governments in Europe?* (pp. 71–92). Brugge: Vanden Broele.

Municipality of Athens (2015) *Programme of Social Policy 2015–2019*, Athens: Municipality of Athens.

Municipality of Heraklion (2013) *Updated Operational Programme 2011–2014*, Heraklion: Municipality of Heraklion

Pejic, D., Acuto, M., and Kosovac, A. (2022) *City Diplomacy during COVID-19: The 2022 Cities and International Engagement Survey*, Melbourne Centre for Cities; Chicago Council on Global Affairs. https://doi.org/10.26188/19719676.

Provan, K.G., and Kenis, P. (2007) "Modes of Network Governance: Structure, Management, and Effectiveness", *Journal of Public Administration Research and Theory*, 18, pp. 229–252.

Radaelli, C. (2000) "Policy Transfer in the European Union: Institutional Isomorphism as a Source of Legitimacy", *Governance*, 13 (1), pp. 25–43.

Stone, D. (2004) "Tranfer Agents and Global Networks in the 'Transnationalization' of Policy", *Journal of European Public Policy*, 11 (3), pp. 545–566.

Tedesco, C. (2010) "EU and Urban Regeneration 'Good Practices' Exchange: From Download to Upload Europeanisation?". In A. Hamedinger and A. Wolffhardt (Eds.) *The Europeanisation of Cities-Policies, Urban Change & Urban Networks* (pp. 183–195). Amsterdam: Techne Press.

Turrini, A., Cristofoli, D., Frosini, F., and Nasi, G. (2010) "Networking Literature about Determinants of Network Effectiveness", *Public Administration*, 88 (2), pp. 528–550.

Van der Pluijm, R., and Melissen, J. (2007) *City Diplomacy: The Expanding Role of Cities in International Politics*, Clingendael: Netherlands Institute of International Relations.

Van Ewijk, E., and Baud, I.S.A. (2009) "Partnerships between Dutch Municipalities and Municipalities in Countries of Migration to the Netherlands; Knowledge Exchange and Mutuality", *Habitat International*, 33 (2), pp. 218–226.

Ward, S., and Williams, R. (1997) "From Hierarchy to Networks? Sub-Central Government and EU Urban Environment Policy", *Journal of Common Market Studies*, 35 (3), pp. 439–464.

Waterhout, B., and Stead, D. (2007) "Mixed Messages: How the ESDP's Concepts Have Been Applied in INTERREG IIIB Programmes, Priorities and Projects", *Planning Practice and Research*, 22 (3), pp. 395–415.

Wilson, G., and Johnson, H. (2007) "Knowledge, Learning and Practice in North-South Practitioner-to-Practitioner Municipal Partnerships", *Local Government Studies*, 33 (2), pp. 253–269.

Index

For Product Safety Concerns and Information please contact our EU
representative GPSR@taylorandfrancis.com
Taylor & Francis Verlag GmbH, Kaufingerstraße 24, 80331 München, Germany